# THE WAY OF JESUS

### A Reflection on the Beatitudes

Published in 2016 by Connor Court Publishing Pty Ltd as a Modotti Press title.

Modotti Press is an imprint of Connor Court Publishing Pty Ltd

Copyright © Fr Ken Barker MGL

All rights reserved. No part of this book may be reproduced or transmitted in any form or by any means, electronic or mechanical, including photocopying, recording or by any information storage and retrieval system, without prior permission in writing from the publisher.

Connor Court Publishing Pty Ltd.
PO Box 7257
Redland Bay QLD 4165
sales@connorcourt.com
www.connorcourt.com
Phone 0497 900 685

ISBN: 978-1-925501-08-7

Nihil Obstat
Rev Warrick Tonkin BA, Dip Ed, Bth, BTheol, M.Ed
Censor Deputatis

Imprimatur
Most Rev Christopher Prowse DD STD
Archbishop of Canberra and Goulburn

Bible quotations taken from the New Revised Standard Version, used with permission

I wish to thank Selina Hasham who examined the text thoroughly, and to Lawrence Yuen for the cover design. Also I have a deep sense of gratitude to my MGL brothers who allowed me the space to be able to bring the manuscript to completion.

Cover design by Br Lawrence Yuen MGL

# Beatitudes in Matthew's Gospel

Blessed are the poor in spirit, for theirs is the kingdom of God.

Blessed are the meek for they will inherit the earth.

Blessed are those who mourn, for they will be comforted.

Blessed are those who hunger and thirst for righteousness, for they will be filled.

Blessed are the merciful, for they will receive mercy.

Blessed are the pure of heart, for they will see God.

Blessed are the peacemakers, for they will be called children of God.

Blessed are those who are persecuted for righteousness' sake, for theirs is the kingdom of heaven.

Blessed are you when people revile you and persecute you and utter all kinds of evil against you falsely on my account. Rejoice and be glad, for your reward is great in heaven, for in the same way they persecuted the prophets who were before you. (Mt 5: 3-11)

# Beatitudes in Luke's Gospel

Blessed are you who are poor, for yours is the kingdom of God.

Blessed are you who are hungry now, for you will be filled.

Blessed are you who weep now, for you will laugh.

Blessed are you when people hate you, and when they exclude you, revile you, and defame you on account of the Son of Man. Rejoice in that day and leap for joy, for surely your reward is great in heaven; for that is what their ancestors did to the prophets.

But woe to you who are rich, for you have received your consolation.

Woe to you who are full now, for you will be hungry.

Woe to you who are laughing now, for you will mourn and weep.

Woe to you when all speak well of you, for that is what their ancestors did to the false prophets. (Lk 6:20-26)

# Contents

| | |
|---|---|
| Foreword | 7 |
| Introduction | 11 |
| 1 Blessed are the poor in spirit | 21 |
| 2 Blessed are the gentle | 33 |
| 3 Blessed are those who mourn | 45 |
| 4 Blessed are those who hunger and thirst for righteousness | 59 |
| 5 Blessed are the merciful | 73 |
| 6 Blessed are the pure of heart | 89 |
| 7 Blessed are the peacemakers | 105 |
| 8 Blessed are those who are persecuted | 119 |
| Beatitudes as a whole | 135 |
| Endnotes | 145 |

# Foreword

The springtime of Catholic biblical renewal is still happening. Over the past few generations, Christian biblical exegesis and interest in all matters biblical has been tremendously enriched. Encouragement has been given especially at the Second Vatican II Council on biblical renewal. No longer simply for biblical academics, the biblical renewal in more recent times is also conspicuously present on the pastoral level. It is common now to visit parishes that have some form of small group biblical studies available to those eager to deepen their spiritual life. The social media has really helped in this area. Access to international and pastoral speakers on the social media is readily available. It can be available even in the remotest parts of Australia and beyond.

In regards to the study of the Beatitudes, we can no longer say that it is simply of interest to the biblical scholars. Much has been written in a necessarily academic way regarding the Beatitudes, but perhaps less so on a more pastoral level.

This is the genius of this inspiring book by the well-known author and founder of the Missionaries of God's Love, Fr Ken Barker. This new book focuses on his pastoral reflection on the Beatitudes.

Fr Ken Barker's approach is immediately accessible to people at all levels of spiritual growth. His tone is profoundly pastoral and kerygmatic. Scriptures form the very soul of his work. His style is like a form of Lectio Divina. It is meditative and reflective. His approach is anecdotal and eclectic. He uses all sorts of stories coming from the Scriptures, or the Tradition of the Catholic Church, to bring home a fuller pastoral interpretation and appreciation of the centrality of the Lord's Beatitudes.

In the *Catechism of the Catholic Church* the Beatitudes are described as central to our Christian vocation. Here we meet the essential message of Christ's preaching. The Catechism introduces the Beatitudes by stating that

"They take up the promises made to the Chosen People since Abraham. The Beatitudes fulfil the promises by ordering them no longer merely to the possession of a territory, but to the kingdom of heaven."[i]

In the Beatitudes, we meet Jesus face to face. They express the vocation of all believers whose faith is founded on the death and resurrection of the Lord Jesus Himself. The Beatitudes "sustain hope in the midst of tribulations; they proclaim the blessings and rewards already secured, however dimly, for Christ's disciples; they have begun in the lives of the Virgin Mary and all the saints."[ii] Surely, in the Beatitudes we find our Christian vocation and the impetus for our practical response in charity to the world.

Fr Ken Barker takes the Beatitudes one by one and reflects on them at length. His text is peppered with stories of witnesses living out each of the Beatitudes. He is not fussed about the academic differences between Luke's and Matthew's versions of the Beatitudes. His purpose is more pastoral.

Fr Barker wishes to lead us close to the Heart of Jesus. From this conversion experience of God's loving mercy, we are assisted in living out the Gospel in our everyday life.

To achieve this aim, Fr Barker has no hesitation in drawing on the insights almost at random from our Christian Tradition. Alongside quotes from St Paul, St Augustine, St Ignatius Loyola, St John Vianney, St Charles de Foucauld, St Francis of Assisi, St Mother Teresa of Calcutta, St John Paul II and Pope Francis, we also read many other testimonials of the Beatitudes. The text of Fr Barker's reflections make us want to stop and reflect on the stories he has just brought to our attention. We want to see the lives of the saints reflected in our own experience as well.

You will find in this book not only reflections from our rich Catholic Tradition over the last 2000 years, but also references to more contemporary witnesses to Christ's presence in the midst of the darkness of our own very fragile society.

Here, for example, Fr Barker reflects on stories coming from the Rwanda genocide of 1994, the more recent turmoils of the Christian communities in Mosul, Iraq and his own personal reflections on conflict resolutions in his everyday priestly life. This approach assists us to try to find linkages between the Beatitudes and happenings in our own life and society. Fr Barker makes this vitally important connection easier with the ease in which he moves from the scriptural text and the spiritual passage, to more recent examples. It helps the Beatitudes to come alive in our own present time!

My hope is that this book will be well read and distributed. It could be used for private spiritual reading, but could also be used in small groups. For example, they could take one of Fr Barkers' chapters and then reflect on its insights for those gathered in prayer. This will ultimately be a wonderful contribution that this book makes.

We thank Fr Barker once again for the courage and the capacity to be able to share his profound spiritual life with us all.

Archbishop Christopher Prowse
Archbishop of Canberra and Goulburn

# Introduction

## True Happiness

The beatitudes have a vital life-changing message for everyone. Jesus provides the ultimate formula for a happy life during our earthly journey, and forever. Blessed are the poor, the gentle, those who mourn and who thirst for righteousness. Blessed also are the merciful, the pure of heart, the peace-makers, and those persecuted for their faith. Jesus invites us to a new-found joy, a state of being in which we are fulfilled and authentically happy.

At some point in life's journey we find ourselves asking, "Am I really happy?" and "What do I need to be genuinely happy?" Usually when these questions arise we are thinking about how we feel. Do I have positive feelings, buoyant emotions, or am I feeling down and depressed, and sad about life? Feelings can be good indicators, but they don't determine happiness. Genuinely happy people can in fact feel quite lousy at certain times when things go wrong and projects become pear-shaped. But that doesn't strip them of their happiness. The psalmist says:

> What can bring us happiness?' many say. Lift up the light of your face on us, O Lord. You have put into my heart a greater joy than they have from abundance of corn and new wine (Ps 4:7-8).

In other words, the quest for happiness is answered in God. We are created for union with him. That is why the face of Jesus is on the front page of this book. As the psalmist says elsewhere, "It is your face, O Lord, that I seek; hide not your face" (Ps 27:8). And again, "Let your face shine on us, O Lord, and we shall be saved" (Numb 6:26). True joy is found in contemplating the face of the Lord, now even if it is "through a glass darkly" (1Cor 13:12), and in heaven when we shall see him fully face to face. As St Augustine famously said, "You have created us for you, O Lord, and our hearts are restless until they rest in you." This is not only longing for eternal rest in heaven, but for true joy now. The promise of the beatitudes is for meaningful living now since if we live the way of Jesus we are fulfilling our deepest purpose as human beings. True happiness comes when our hearts are in love with God, and hence moving in love for others.

The psalmist laments, "O, how long will your hearts be closed, will you love what is futile and seek what is false?" (Ps 4:3) To fall in love with what is useless and to give one's heart to the illusory attractions of this world is the way to *lose* beatitude; it is the formula for *un*happiness. Some people think that wealth will bring happiness, others self-indulgent pleasure, others power, others prestige and fame. But these aspirations in themselves will ultimately leave us empty and unfulfilled. When we let any created reality, even good things, become a god for us, we lose our bearings as human beings, and are left with a gnawing emptiness within the heart that is never satisfied. Human beings are created for love. God is love. We only find genuine happiness in the love of God.

In the prevailing culture we have a fascination with celebrities who have "made it", but all too often we then witness the tragic outcome of their foolish decisions, as their lives unravel out of control. How easy it is for the human heart to be deceived about what will bring true happiness! It dreams for more material things, to get to the top of one's profession, to become a star in sport or music or scientific exploration, or in whatever one's passion is. Of course it is good to aspire to higher things and to desire greatness. But the critical question we must ask is "what sort of greatness?" We will only find our true greatness as human beings when we discover ourselves in God and begin to live out our God-given destiny. When the disciples were arguing about who was the greatest, Jesus told them "Whoever wants to be first, must be last of all and servant of all" (Mk 9:35). That puts a curve into our pleasure-seeking, ambitious dreams! It is a call to self-sacrificing love which is *the* highest aspiration of the human being. If someone goes through life and fails to genuinely love, then it is a life not worth living.

The beatitudes, unforgettably proclaimed on the mountain by Jesus, are his persuasive invitation to discover his way of love, and hence attain our destiny. They call us to the greatness of genuine discipleship. They call us to the blessedness God intended for us. They call us to the freedom of loving others as Jesus loved. They offer us the formula for a life of peace and joy.

The natural desire for happiness planted in us by God's creative love can only be fulfilled by God. We are called to blessedness, to participate fully in the life of God. Our lives are not meant to end up on the scrap heap as a result of excessive indulgence, slavery to riches, and captivity to selfish passions. Nor are our lives meant to be a tedious treadmill of religious mediocrity. We are meant for union with God and to grow in his heart of love. By grace we can cooperate with God's purpose for us and become who we are truly called to be.

## Abundant Joy Now and Forever

The promise of Jesus is that we become "blessed". The Greek word is *makarios*. It means the happiness of heaven where we are fulfilled as human beings and share in the joy of God. Jesus promises this joyful life now, but because of our imperfections we are not yet capable of receiving it in fullness. The completion of this happiness will ultimately come in heaven. But the good news proclaims that if we are growing in living the beatitudes now, we *already* experience heaven. The kingdom of God dwells within us 'already' but is 'not yet' brought to completion.

The beatitudes are not pious dreams or wishful thinking about a world that could come in some distant future. They are a celebration of what already is. They are exclamations from Jesus about the kingdom of God which is already beginning to take hold in the heart of his disciples. Jesus began his ministry proclaiming, "The time has come the kingdom of God is at hand, repent and believe the good news" (Mk1:15). As people begin to respond to the gift of the kingdom, their hearts are converted, and their lives changed, showing the good fruit of the beatitudes. They have already entered blessedness. It is a present reality. Jesus exclaims, "O the blessedness of the poor in spirit!" "O the blessedness of the gentle!" and so on. In celebrating what was already taking place, Jesus was also inviting others who had not yet opened their hearts to him to do so and receive the same blessedness.

"Blessedness" is the joy in the heart of Jesus, which he imparts to his disciples. It is the joy of knowing the unconditional love of God and allowing God's love to take hold in our lives. It is the joy of the kingdom of God. Jesus is saying in effect, "O the joy of being a disciple! O the joy of following me and living according to my way! O the sheer happiness of knowing me as your Master, Saviour and Lord!" The beatitudes are an invitation into the joy of the Father's house.

As we listen to the beatitudes it would be a mistake to hear them as solely good moral instruction from a wise teacher. This is the way they have been received by many who have not met Jesus personally. The beatitudes are much more than this. They articulate what happens to the soul when we meet Jesus. They are a statement of the joy of being Christian. Jesus promised his followers that after his resurrection we would be given "a joy that no one will take from you" (Jn 16:22). Christian joy cannot be extinguished. It is completely unassailable. The martyrs witness to this reality most powerfully. It is a joy that shines through tears, a joy that cannot be lost, no matter how much pain and sorrow, or how much calamity and misfortune. In proclaiming the beatitudes Jesus is fulfilling the words of the prophet, "Go up on a high mountain, joyful messenger to Zion. Shout with a loud voice joyful messenger to Jerusalem" (Is 40:9). Jesus himself "rejoiced in the Holy Spirit" (Lk 10:21), and his message on the mountain brings joy, "I have said these things to you, so that my joy may be in you, and that your joy may be complete" (Jn 15:11).

## Promise of Eternal Joy

We have beatitude now, but it is yet to come in fullness. All the promises given to Abraham are now taken up to a new level. Abraham was promised land and descendants as many as the stars in the sky and sands on the seashore. But the promise of Jesus goes beyond this. It is the promise of the blessedness of the eternal kingdom of God. All the eight promises of the beatitudes are for the present life, but even more so for the future life when we depart this earth through death and enter eternity. There is a secret longing for eternity in every person. We are made for this. Most people these days have little or no concept of eternity. They do not know their destiny. This means they cannot appreciate the full import of the beatitudes.

Secularists will often claim that eternity is an invention of people who don't take this life seriously, and consequently look for an illusory escape to come. To the contrary, we, who proclaim eternity is real, find this life on earth so precious we cannot conceive of it ending in nothing. Through faith in Jesus, we have come to know the joy of eternal life here and now. Having tasted of the banquet of life we are yearning for the fullness yet to come. The person who has not found the meaning of life now, will be indifferent about its ending. But those who know God cannot imagine that the goodness of what we experience now would end in a black hole of nothingness. We know that when our earthly pilgrimage ends we enter into life forever with God – the bliss of heaven. This is the promise of the beatitudes.

## The Heart of Jesus

With a cheeky play on words we may call them the "be-attitudes"; attitudes of heart which spring from our being in God. They are not rules to which we conform, or external actions which we can put on like our clothes in the morning. Nor are they a set of principles or a theory about what is good for human beings. Jesus' preaching on the mountain is a call to conversion of the heart. The heart is the deepest level of the human person, the source from which flows all thoughts, feelings, attitudes and actions. For Jesus, it is the heart that matters. The beatitudes tell us about the qualities of the human heart of Jesus, and hence about the qualities of heart of his genuine disciples.

Pope Benedict says the beatitudes portray "a veiled interior biography of Jesus, a kind of portrait of his figure."[1] The Catechism concurs: "they depict the countenance of Jesus Christ and portray his charity."[2] Jesus is speaking from the heart and is calling us to have his heart and to be like him. The beatitudes are not just moral injunctions but first and foremost they are a self-description of Jesus; how he is as a human being, the most attractive and compelling figure who ever walked the face of the earth. They call us to aim at imitating him.

## The Way of Discipleship

If we want to follow Jesus we will allow the Holy Spirit to fill us and bring us into union with him. John reminds us, "If we claim to be living in Christ then we should be living as he lived. Whoever says 'I abide in him' ought to walk just as he walked" (1 Jn 2:6). Over time we will become gradually transformed more into his likeness. The only perfect human being is Christ himself, and only he is fully blessed. But to the degree that we allow him to rule in our lives by his love we can be changed into his likeness, and begin to experience the bliss of heaven.

Paul encourages the Ephesians to "put away your former way of life, your old self, corrupted and deluded by its lusts" (Eph 4:20-22). They must not fall back into their old pagan ways, with no sense of right and wrong, and abandon themselves to all sorts of immoral behaviour. He says that is not "the way you learnt Christ". What does he mean to "learn Christ"? It means to be conformed to Christ, having the same mind and same attitudes as Christ, making the same decisions as Christ, and living as he did. "For anyone who is in Christ there is a new creation; everything old has passed away: see, everything has become new" (2Cor 5:17). The beatitudes give us a clear down to earth picture of what this looks like. Being holy is not about being pious or sanctimonious. It is about being like Jesus, and there is no better description of this way of holiness than the beatitudes.

The beatitudes are not goals to be accomplished by our hard work alone. Jesus is not saying we will be blessed *because* we do good works, as if it all depended on our efforts. No, all is grace, sheer gift from God. By choosing to be poor in spirit, gentle and pure of heart, merciful, and peacemakers, we are cooperating with the grace of God. Our cooperation is essential. As Augustine wistfully remarked, "The God who made us without our cooperation will not save us without our cooperation." Living the beatitudes is a response to God's unconditional love for us. All is a work of grace. But we must allow ourselves to be shaped into his likeness, letting the Spirit of God change us, so the fruits of the Spirit will become more evident in our behaviour. In this way we become true Christians. We let the mind of Christ be within us. We come to know the gift of real blessedness.

## Witness to Jesus

The beatitudes are the most authentic and convincing summary of living the good news in the way of Jesus. The light of Jesus shines in the world through the joy of his disciples when they live the beatitudes. After the resurrection the disciples were filled with this unadulterated joy. Wherever they went they brought "great joy" to the people (Acts 8:8) and even in the midst of persecution they continued to be "filled with joy" (Acts 13:52). We are called first to live the gospel radically with joyful hearts, and then proclaim the gospel joyfully with authority. Others must experience us as good news first, and then our words will be convincing.

Through our wordless witness people will ask questions, "Why are they like this? Where do they get this joy from? Why do they live this way? What or who is it that inspires them? Why are they in our midst?"[3] People today will be influenced first by our witness before our words, and if they are influenced by our words it will be because of our witness.[4] As St Paul told his communities we are the "aroma of Christ". By living the beatitudes joyfully we exude the perfume of Christ (2Cor 2:14). People are irresistibly attracted to Christ. We witness by attraction, not by proselytising.

The Church community should be known most by the way it lives the beatitudes. Thomas Aquinas included the beatitudes in his teaching on morality, but he distinguished them from the commandments. They presume the commandments; but they are ideals that go beyond the law. The Christian community must not only declare the law of God and witness to keeping the law. We need to live the higher ideal, showing the "sweetness" of the fruits of the Spirit. We are to witness to the joy of living the beatitudes.

## A Challenge to the Way of the World

The way of Jesus challenges the prevailing attitudes and behaviour of the world. The beatitudes turn the standards of the world upside down. They proclaim the values of the kingdom of God, which are in conflict with the worldly attitudes. So those who are poor in worldly terms are the ones who are the fortunate ones, those who suffer much are blessed and are joyful in their afflictions, those who choose not to be aggressive but gentle shall inherit the earth, those who forgive the unjust aggressor are rewarded, those who are persecuted for their faith will rejoice.

Those who live the beatitudes no longer invest in this world's agenda. They are but pilgrims in this earthly sojourn. They don't fall down before the contemporary idols, but keep their hearts set on the world that will never end. They are pilgrims, moving purposefully towards their heavenly homeland. The beatitudes teach them a new way to live now during this short time on earth, and empowers them to reach their destiny in God.

## Two Accounts: Matthew and Luke

We have two accounts of the beatitudes, one in Matthew's gospel which is the more commonly known, and one in Luke's gospel which adds extra punch to what is found in Matthew. To gain the full picture of what Jesus preached we need to look at both. In Matthew's gospel the beatitudes are placed at the beginning of the Sermon on the Mount, which is stylised as the teaching of the new Moses. Just as Moses went up the mountain to receive the old covenant commandments, now Jesus goes up the mountain and, seated as a master teacher, delivers new moral teachings which don't abolish the old law but fulfil it.

Luke's account has Jesus on the "plain", not the mountain. He starts his proclamation by "fixing his eyes on his disciples." So while the crowds are present, and all are meant to hear, Jesus directs his attention especially to his disciples. Jesus is looking upon his disciples and describing their actual situation. They are poor, weeping, hated and persecuted. Because of this they are fortunate; they are blessed.

In this book we are primarily following Matthew's account, but we will also include Luke's perspective when we are dealing with the four particular beatitudes which he highlights, and also the four accompanying woes. This is with the conviction that both accounts originated from the same literary source, and that the different shades of meaning enrich our understanding. While some argue for Luke and some for Matthew, I believe that the perspectives of the two evangelists are compatible, and that a synthesis of the two accounts is possible.

# 1
# BLESSED ARE THE POOR IN SPIRIT

*Blessed are the poor in spirit for theirs is the kingdom of heaven Mt 5:3*

## An Attitude of Heart

To be poor in spirit is a fundamental attitude of heart. In the gospel the Greek word "*ptokoi*" is used for "poor ones". It means to be utterly destitute. But let's not be mistaken. Jesus is not sanctifying unwanted destitution. How could that be a blessing to anyone? We need to be clear that this beatitude is not describing a socio-economic group. Rather, it is calling us to a new attitude. Jesus is addressing each and every one of us. We are being asked by the Lord to become radically aware of our nothingness before God. We are the creatures; he is the Creator. Without him we are "destitute". It is an invitation to discover more really our absolute poverty before God. We are to recognise our utter vulnerability and total dependence on God. We become blessed if we accept our state as creatures and don't deny this truth as Adam and Eve did.

Without poverty in spirit everything goes wrong. This was the original fault of Adam and Eve. In the garden of Eden they refused to trust the promise of God, and listened rather to the promise of Satan. They tried to take control of things themselves. Disaster followed. Another image of the Fall in Genesis is the story of the tower of Babel. Arrogantly, humanity tried to build a tower to the heavens, overreaching human limitations. The attempt failed in an irrevocable breakdown in human communication. This ancient story describes the situation in today's world. Due to pride and arrogance, our communion with one another has become dislocated. While science and technology can do much to help us, if we rely absolutely on their capacity to build a better world we are doomed to failure. But when we are poor in spirit and accept our limitations as creatures, bowing in adoration before God, we will build a world community to God's glory.

We human beings are born poor; we are poor; and we die poor. We come into the world with nothing, we are meant to live holding on to nothing, and we die with nothing. Sometimes the Lord allows a catastrophe to happen in our lives to bring this truth home. One fateful day a sudden fire broke out in the building where my office was located. I had stored there much of the research work I had done over years, irreplaceable documents, and other articles of more sentimental value. Within a few minutes years of work went up in smoke, with no back-up to recover it. Later, I was allowed to enter the building. Standing in the charred remains, feeling stripped of everything, by the grace of God the prayer of Job arose in my heart, "Naked I came from my mother's womb, naked I shall return. The Lord has given and the Lord has taken away. Blessed be the name of the Lord" (Job 1:21). It was a blessing for me to be reduced to nothing.

Our poverty is not only due to our humble state as creatures, but also because we are wounded from the original sin. We are dis-functional creatures. Since the original Fall of humanity we have not been able to come to wholeness. There has been a basic flaw in our being. This is the poverty of our brokenness, our proneness to sin, the fault-line in our being, liable to cause a seismic upheaval at any time. We walk in our utter need for the Saviour. And thanks be to God for Jesus Christ who became one of us, and shared in our poverty, so that he could save us. "Though he was rich, for our sakes he became poor, so that by his poverty we might become rich" (2Cor 8: 9-10). He entered into our condition of sinfulness without sinning; he took upon himself the consequences of our sin. Emptying himself of his divinity, he became like we are except for sin, and he emptied himself even further by being stripped of everything on the Cross, so that we could be enriched with new life. When we walk honestly in our true poverty we rely totally upon his saving power.

# Detachment of Heart

The only authentic way to walk through these few short years on this earth is to hold onto nothing, so that we can hold onto God and be held by him. This is the attitude of detachment. When our hearts are free we can discover love. Jesus offered this precious gift to the young man in the gospel who ran up to him, fell at his feet and asked what must he do for eternal life. At first Jesus instructed him to keep the commandments. The young man blurted out that he had always kept them since he was a child. Then Jesus "looked steadily at him and loved him" (Mk 10: 17-22). He wanted to call this young man to the greater thing. Jesus could see that this man's wealth had a hold on his heart. He needed to let go of this inordinate attachment so he would be free to love. Hence the challenge from Jesus: "There is one thing you lack. Go sell what you own, and give the money to the poor, and you will have treasure in heaven. Then come, follow me." The man went away sad and depressed. Out of fear of becoming miserable without his wealth, he actually became the most miserable figure of all.

The poor in spirit are blessed because they are free from any attachment which would hold the heart captive, preventing them from being in union with God. I heard once how in some parts of India hunters catch monkeys. They put a hole in a large, heavy clay pot, just big enough for the monkey's hand to go through. Inside the pot they put nuts and berries that monkeys like. The monkey comes along and senses there is something special in the pot. He puts his hand through the hole and grabs it to his delight. Then he tries to pull out his hand to eat his newly found treasure; but the fist is too large for him to withdraw his hand! All the silly monkey has to do is let go of the food, but he doesn't want to lose it. After much frustrated squealing and antics from the monkey, the hunters come along and pick him up and take him off to the circus. All the monkey had to do was to let go, but he wouldn't. The Holy Spirit shows us what has a hold on our heart in such a way that we are not free for the kingdom of God. Jesus promises the blessings of the kingdom if we let go and allow him to reign in our hearts. His rule is one of love, but he cannot claim the territory of the heart if we are still holding tightly to anything other than him.

St Ignatius Loyola teaches about this grace of detachment. He starts his spiritual exercises with the fundamental principle and foundation of our life: that God alone is our ultimate end. Everything in our lives must be a means towards that end. We have been created to love, honour and serve God here on earth and to be forever with him in heaven. This means that we must not have any inordinate attachment to anything in such a way that it becomes an absolute for us. Everything needs to be subordinate to the one purpose – to give glory to God. It is a call to be detached from all things of this world – honour, status, money, power, achievements, health, the length of my life, the manner of my death, my loved ones – all that I may hold dear. We need to cultivate an attitude of "holy indifference", even when it comes to our plans for the future, or the decisions we are making, or the spiritual ideals and dreams we cherish. Ignatius, who founded the Jesuits, was once asked how he would cope if the Pope ordered his congregation to disband. His answer was, "I would need a short time in the chapel, and then I would be fine". In other words, he would need time to give it over to the Lord, and then he would be at peace. I once was watching Mother Teresa being interviewed about a convent of hers which the local authorities had decided to reclaim. The reporter was asking how she felt about it. Her response was simple, but profound. Referring to the Lord she replied, "I take what he gives; and give what he takes". That is poverty of spirit.

The poor in spirit know that everything is gift from God. They walk through life with a profound sense of gratitude which is the way to humility. When we are grateful we recognise that God is the source of all the gifts of creation and salvation. On the other hand, when we are ungrateful, we complain about our lot and pine for what others have. We fall into envy of others' gifts and possessions. Francis of Assisi warns that envy is next to blasphemy; since it does not recognise God as the author of all gifts and that God bestows his gifts as he pleases. So the spiritually poor ones are trusting in the providence of God at all times. They have the heart of Jesus, who said to his disciples "not to worry about your life and what you are to eat, nor about your body and how you are to clothe it" (Lk 12:22-32). He pointed to the birds of the air and the lilies of the field, to see how they are clothed so beautifully. How much more will God look after us! We are not to be anxious about anything; all is in the hands of our loving Father. He knows we need these things. Jesus urges, "set your hearts on his kingdom and these other things will be given as well". We are not to be afraid about our future, nor about provision for our life now. We are in the arms of a loving Father who will never desert us nor disappoint us.

## Voluntary Poverty

So far I have emphasised "poverty of spirit" as given in Mathew's gospel. When we come to Luke's account of the beatitudes there is a shift in focus. While looking at his disciples, Jesus simply says, "Blessed are *you* poor". In this case Jesus is obviously referring to actual material poverty. There was an O.T. tradition of the "poor ones", the *anawim* in Hebrew. These were the people who were "bowed down", "downtrodden", "oppressed", holding no property nor having any influence. Since the poor and oppressed were helpless, with no power or prestige, they had to rely totally upon God for their vindication. Since they have nothing on earth they must trust God totally. However, as I have already indicated, by the time of Jesus this tradition had become more spiritual in meaning – the truly poor are those who come to God with empty hands, open to receiving gifts, relying upon his goodness. Nevertheless, Luke's emphasis shows that spiritual poverty is only authentic if it goes together with a truly simple way of life. It cannot be an interior disposition alone without being expressed in a gospel life style. Rather than rely upon wealth, power and prestige for their security, the poor in spirit live in evangelical frugality and simplicity.

In the Old Testament there was no tradition of voluntarily being poor for the sake of others. Material prosperity was a major sign of God's favour. The prosperous had the duty to care for the poor by giving generously. But there was no call to actually *choose* material poverty as a way of life. Voluntary poverty is a gospel innovation found only in the New Testament. Jesus calls his disciples to adopt it. "None of you can be my disciple if you do not give up all your possessions" (Lk 14: 33). While the O.T. presented a God who is *for* the poor; the N.T. presents a God who *makes himself poor* for our sake. He comes in solidarity with those who are materially poor. While in the O.T. the blessing came with material prosperity; in the N.T. the blessing comes with *being poor* in imitation of Jesus. This is meant to be a feature of anyone responding to the call to holiness. Lay people as well as religious must aspire to follow Jesus in his gospel poverty, but in different ways. Let's turn to the religious first.

## Total Renunciation

Those who are called to renounce all their possessions for the sake of the kingdom become a prophetic sign in the church. When lived faithfully, this consecrated way of life calls the whole church to relativise the goods of this earth and to acknowledge that God alone is our lasting treasure. It is a sign of the kingdom of God to come, witnessing that our ultimate joy is found in God's love. It is like the man in the parable, who found the treasure in the field. He was so filled with joy that he was prepared to sell up everything to purchase the field (Mt 13:44). When we discover the beauty and power of God's love in our lives we look upon worldly realities differently. We are no longer captive to possessions, pleasure, power or fame. God is enough.

Francis, the poor man of Assisi, proclaimed this truth by his way of life. The early accounts of his brotherhood describe men so filled with love of God that nothing else mattered. One of Francis' first followers was Bernard, a young noble of Assisi. He had secretly watched Francis praying through the night, uttering again and again, "My God and my all". By morning Bernard was convinced that this love of God which Francis proclaimed was real.[5] He decided to leave the world and follow Jesus in radical poverty. Upon learning of Bernard's desire Francis decided to discern his calling in a rather creative and unusual way. They went to the church and after praying to the Holy Spirit, Francis opened the Lectionary randomly three times. At the first opening their eyes fell on the invitation of Jesus to the rich young man, "If you want to be perfect, go, sell all you have, and give to the poor, and come, follow me." At the second opening they came upon Jesus sending out the 72 disciples instructing them "Take nothing for your journey, neither staff, nor purse, nor bread, nor money", indicating that their poverty would leave them free for apostolic mission and that they were to live by the Lord's provision. The third time the book fell open on the text, "If anyone wishes to come after me, let him deny himself, and take up his cross, and follow me." Immediately Bernard, who was quite wealthy, went to his house, gathered up all his gold coins, and then joyfully distributed them amongst the poor. That day in the town square there was much excitement and celebration as ordinary people suddenly found themselves holding more money than ever before. But the most joyful ones were Francis and Bernard, who knew that out of love for the Lord they had entered into a new level of freedom for the kingdom of God.

Those who choose radical evangelical poverty become a sign of the coming kingdom by their very way of life. It points towards a time when earthly goods will no longer have any value, but when God will be all in all. It is not a negative attitude towards the good things of God's creation, but simply a way of signifying that this world is passing away. We are but pilgrims on a journey with our hearts set on a world that will never end.

## The Many Ways of Poverty

We need to be careful and prudent in the way we understand the call to gospel poverty. It will take a different shape depending on one's particular vocation. Not everyone will be called to dispossess like Francis and Bernard. Even amongst religious men and women today there are varying degrees of radical evangelical poverty. For lay people who earn money for their living, look after a family, and have many financial responsibilities, it could seem at first glance unreasonable to talk about material poverty. Maybe they should only focus on being poor in spirit. But the gospel does not exempt anyone responding to the call to actual poverty. Although we must remember that Jesus did not give any prescriptive instruction on how to go about this. Each person, each family, each community, is left to discern how they should best respond. Our decisions need to be in the light of the gospel, and with a common sense approach to our own situation. There is nothing inherently wrong with being well endowed financially and living comfortably, but the gospel warning lights go on when we indulge excessively in luxury items, extravagant tastes, and needless opulence.

Jesus warns about the amassing of riches for their own sake. He tells the parable of the man who hoarded his produce in a barn, and then with further success built bigger barns (Lk 12:13-21). He thought to himself, "My soul, you have plenty of good things laid by for many years to come; take things easy, eat, drink, have a good time". He was comfortable and secure according to the world's standards. But God said to him, "Fool! This very night the demand will be made for your soul; and this hoard of yours, whose will it be then?" Our security is not in our material possessions. It is not the way of Jesus to accumulate wealth for its own sake. In today's world where the division between rich and poor is so dramatic, there is a gospel imperative to simplify our life-styles, and renounce affluence and wasteful living. We are called by Jesus to *be* poor and to be *for* the poor. But the balance of these will vary depending on how the Lord calls us.

In contemplating evangelical poverty it helps to notice that Jesus did not become totally destitute. He did not belong to the "poorest of the poor" class of his time. He was a tradesman working for his living and hence had some social status. He was not homeless. Although he did say about himself, "Foxes have holes and the birds of the air nests, but the Son of man has nowhere to lay his head" (Lk 9:58). He was an itinerant preacher with no guaranteed bed, but at times he would have found a bed in one of the villages, while at other times maybe they slept under the stars or in a cave in the Jordan valley. Yet in his public life he was considered a Rabbi and he had wealthy friends. To follow Jesus does not mean necessarily to enter into abject poverty or destitution. But we cannot dismiss the gospel call to poverty. The manner of Jesus' birth, his ordinary way of living, and his style of ministry in no way speaks of material wealth, but rather points towards simplicity and solidarity with the weak, broken and outcast of the society. The poverty of Jesus is found primarily in his *choice* to become poor for our sake out of love for us so we could be set free. The motivation is love.

When, in imitation of Jesus, we simplify our way of life, we do it for love of others. We freely embrace gospel poverty to be in solidarity with those who have much less than we do.

St Paul exclaims, "For his sake I have suffered the loss of all things, and I regard them as rubbish, in order that I may gain Christ." (Phil 3:8). There are some followers of Jesus, in particular consecrated persons, who are called to divest of everything for the Lord and for the kingdom. Others will not feel called to pursue that level of response, but will still heed the call to let go of needless luxuries and choose to be less extravagant in their way of life. Whatever level of poverty we choose, Paul warns us that "If I give away all my possessions, and if give over my body to be burnt, but do not have love, I gain nothing" (1Cor 13:3). We embrace a simple life because of love for Jesus and love for the poor. Otherwise it may be motivated from an unhealthy sense of guilt or a hidden pride. The blessing comes when there is love.

## Woe to You Rich

Coupled with the promise of blessing for those who choose a poor way of life is the warning for those who succumb to riches. "Woe to you who are rich; you are having your consolation now". This is not a condemnation of wealth as such, but a warning that "it is easier for a camel to go through the eye of a needle than for someone who is rich to enter the kingdom of God" (Mk 10:25). Possessions can possess the heart and stifle any movement towards God. It is not just a matter of sharing what we have with the poor, but of simplifying our lives in solidarity with the poor. The parable of the rich man and Lazarus comes to mind (Lk 16:19-31). The rich man dressed in purple, a sign of opulence, feasted sumptuously every day. The poor man, Lazarus, who was covered with sores, indicating his dereliction, was denied even the scraps from the rich man's table. Even the dogs gave him some comfort by licking his sores, but he received no comfort from the rich man. The sin of the rich man is indifference, insulating himself from the plight of the poor man at his door. But after death the tables are turned. Now the poor man has the eternal comfort of "Abraham's bosom", the consolation of God, and the rich man is in torment, crying out for relief from his agony. But it is too late. That is the meaning of the words, "Woe to you who are rich; you are having your consolation now". This consolation of the rich will not last, and in eternity it will be a very different story.

## Idolatory of Money

Jesus makes it very clear: "No one can serve two masters; for a slave will either hate the one and love the other, or be devoted to the one and despise the other. You cannot serve both God and wealth" (Mt 6:24). We can turn money into an idol and bow before it as the "golden calf". Money gives human beings an illusory sense of power: "You can do anything if you have money". It creates the deception of self-sufficiency and shuts out the life of God. Scripture says, "The love of money is a root of all kinds of evil" (1Tim 6:10). This is no exaggeration. Greed is at the heart of so much misery in the world — drug dealing, human trafficking, war, terrorism, homelessness, world hunger — whatever the misery, if we dig deep, we find an underlying pursuit of money. Money is a false god which captures the human heart and shuts people out of the kingdom of God.

Jesus warns the rich to escape from the danger that assails them. "Do not store up for yourselves treasures on earth, where moth and rust consume and where thieves break in and steal. But store up for yourselves treasures in heaven, where neither moth nor rust consumes and thieves do not break in and steal. For where your treasure is, there your heart will be also" (Mt 6:19-21). So rather than bury their riches in some bank vault why not use their wealth for the kingdom of God? Rather than using their riches to become more wealthy, why not put it in the service of good. Certainly this can be achieved by generously giving to projects that help the poor, but also possibly by initiating new ways of doing business that enable others to participate in the blessing of their wealth. Timothy says, "As for those who, in the present age, are rich ...They are to do good, to be rich in good works, generous and ready to share, thus storing up for themselves the treasure of a good foundation for the future, so that they may take hold of the life that really is life" (1Tim 6:17-19).

Recently Pope Francis issued a pressing appeal to the World Economic Forum held in Davos, Switzerland.[6] His message to government ministers from 100 countries and 1,500 CEOs of the most important companies was a heartfelt plea: "Do not forget the poor!". He urged the participants, "Do not be afraid to open your minds and hearts to the poor. In this way, you will give free rein to your economic and technical talents, and discover the happiness of a full life, which consumerism of itself cannot provide." He continued, "We must never allow the culture of prosperity to deaden us, to make us incapable of feeling compassion at the outcry of the poor, of weeping for other people's pain, and of sensing the need to help them, as if this was someone else's responsibility and not our own." He makes it clear that responsibility for the poor is "an essential part of our humanity", and having compassion for the poor involves accepting that our "own actions can be a cause of injustice and inequality".

## Preferential Option for the Poor

There is a special place in the heart of God for the poor. This has implications for our mission as Church. God came to us in poverty. He was born in a stable in Bethlehem, shut out from the inn. He lay in swaddling clothes in a manger, which was a feeding trough for animals. He was presented in the Temple along with two turtledoves, the offering that people made who could not afford a lamb. He grew up in a humble carpenter's shop, working with his hands and earning his keep. While he was not destitute he certainly was in touch with the lowly and less fortunate of the society. When Jesus said, "Blessed are you poor" he "assured those burdened by sorrow and crushed by poverty that God has a special place for them in his heart."[7]

As Church we seek to have the attitude of the heart of God, and so our mission is primarily to the poor. We are to be a Church *of* the poor and *for* the poor. This is not some nice idea with leftish leanings, but the heart of the Church's mission based on our faith in Christ. It is not so much a call to more programs of assistance, although these are important. Rather it requires a change of heart, a sort of conversion to the poor, whereby we gain a new awareness that we are one with the least in the society, those on the peripheries who are usually overlooked and discarded. Pope Francis speaks of a "loving attentiveness" to the poor – an attitude which is free of condescension and esteems the personal dignity of the other. It means entering into friendship with the poor, rather than simply bestowing "hand outs". We find that the poor have so much to offer us. "We let ourselves be evangelized by them … to find Christ in them, to lend our voice to their causes, but also to be their friends, to listen to them, to speak for them and to embrace the mysterious wisdom which God wishes to share with us through them."[8]

# 2
# BLESSED ARE THE GENTLE[9]

*Blessed are the meek, for they will inherit the earth Mt 5:4*

The promise of Jesus is that the gentle will inherit the land. The Greek word used is *"praus"*, which is sometimes translated as "meek". The word carries within it the idea of humility of heart, and patience in the face of opposition or adversity. Jesus himself is the model. He calls all who "labour and are heavy burdened" to come to him to find rest for their souls. He says, "learn from me for I am gentle (meek) and humble of heart" (Mt 11:29). This tenderness in the heart of Jesus is his most attractive feature. He meets us where we hurt most, and when we are most oppressed by life's troubles. We find comfort and healing in his gentle embrace of love and mercy. He is the one who "does not break the crushed reed nor quench the wavering flame" (Mt 12: 19-20 cf. Is 42:2-3). Following on from John the Baptist he shows us the "tender mercy of the heart of our God who has come to visit us like the dawn from on high" (Lk 1:78).

## King of Peace

Down through the ages kings, tyrants and despots have tried to conquer the world by military might, but they have only succeeded in adding to the rubble heap of history due to the scourge of war. In this futile endeavour no one wins. In war all are losers. One war finishes, they take a rest for a while, wounds are healed, fears forgotten, and then they are at it again. This time they think victory will be achieved and we will have lasting peace. It is an illusion; sheer madness. In this context the voice of Jesus of Nazareth echoes from the mountainside above the sea of Galilee: "Blessed are the gentle; they will inherit the earth." The world will not be conquered by force of arms or political pressure. The world will be won by love. Jesus chose not to call down legions of angels to destroy the perpetrators of violence and conquer evil. He came to win the earth with meekness.

When Jesus entered Jerusalem he was riding on a donkey. This was no accident. The prophet Zechariah had prophesied it would be this way. Matthew tells us it took place to fulfil the prophecy, "Look, your king comes to you; he is humble (gentle), he rides on a donkey" (Mt 21:4-5 cf Zech 9:9-10). He is not on a war horse, but a humble ass. He is not violent like earthly kings; his rule does not depend on political or military might. He is King of peace. The prophecy continues, "his dominion shall be from sea to sea, and from the river to the ends of the earth". Yes, it is a universal kingdom which will be accomplished without one shot being fired; it will be the rule of hearts won by the gentleness of Jesus found in his followers. God's claim on the earth is universal, and the earth belongs ultimately to the meek and gentle of heart.

## Patience in Suffering

When Jesus was arrested and arraigned before Caiaphas, and then Pilate, there was no anger, retaliation or vengeance. "When he was insulted, he did not insult in return: when he was tortured, he did not threaten" (1Pet 2:23). He builds his kingdom by renouncing violence and accepting suffering. In John's account of the passion when Jesus was slapped in the face by the servant of the High Priest he did not retaliate. He simply spoke the truth and challenged the injustice of what had been done: "If there is something wrong in what I have said point it out; but if there is no offence in it why do you strike me?" (Jn 18;23)

But the most startling thing about his response to the cruel treatment during the passion is his silence. He endures his suffering patiently. When he does speak it is with mercy. In Luke's gospel when Jesus is being nailed to the Cross and lightning bolts of agonising pain were shooting through his whole nervous system he cried out, "Father, forgive them, for they know not what they do" (Lk 23:40). He was willing to absorb all the pain into himself and let it die there. As Peter continues, "He was bearing our faults in his own body on the cross, so that we might die to our faults and live for holiness; through his wounds we have been healed" (1Pet 2:24). Jesus teaches us that true greatness is not established by violence and subjugation of our enemies, but by self-abasement and service of others.

## Gentle When Opposed

When a Samaritan town refused to welcome Jesus, the disciples wanted him to bring down fire upon the town to punish and destroy them. This is not the way of Jesus. He rebuked his disciples and went to another village. We must be meek in the face of persecution for the sake of the gospel. The proclamation of the gospel is never served by anger, bitterness, condemnation and contempt. When the enemies of the good news come against us we must dig deep and find a Christ-like heart which meets the attack with meekness. Paul encouraged Timothy, a young man seemingly given to hot-headed debates with his adversaries: "Have nothing to do with stupid and senseless controversies; you know they breed quarrels. And the Lord's servant must not be quarrelsome, but kindly to everyone, a good teacher, and patient, correcting opponents with gentleness" (2Tim 2: 23-25). Ultimately our strident argumentation will not win the day; rather the kindness of our character will. Gentleness is persuasive; polemical wrangling repels. We want to be able to bring people to salvation, not to leave them in endless disputation.

We move in gentleness in proclaiming the gospel. Peter encourages, "In your hearts reverence Christ as the Lord. Always be prepared to give an account of the hope that is within you. Yet do it with gentleness (*prautes*, meekness) and reverence" (1Pet 3:15). We are seeking to win the hearts of human beings, not just to win a debate, no matter how important the issue at stake. People will read *us* first, and if they perceive an intolerant, condemning person it feeds the stereotypical image they already have of "Christians", which is propagated in the popular culture. Unfortunately, in today's society Christians can have bad press and an unattractive image because, rightly or wrongly, they appear to others as speaking words of damnation rather than words of hope. A person with a gentle heart is irresistible. We are to be the image of Christ, his face in the world today. People need to encounter the gentleness of Christ. Surely we must speak the truth, but what is most important is to "speak the truth *in love*" (Eph 4:15). This is particularly difficult when we are under hostile attack in the public sphere and also when many of our associates are quick to ridicule what the Church believes and teaches. But the promise of Jesus is that "the meek will inherit the earth". There is no doubt about this.

## Win Others by Gentleness

In sixteenth century Geneva, and the surrounding Chablais district, which was almost exclusively occupied by Calvinists, there was a highly intolerant anti-Catholic environment. A young priest, Francis de Sales, was given the task to make his way into this territory and win people back to the Catholic faith. Before him others had failed miserably to win the people through messages of fear and condemnation. Francis' aim was simply to persuade the people by love. His gentleness won the day. Rather than engage in a frontal attack he would personally befriend significant leaders and in the course of trustful conversation speak the truth in love. In the heat of post-Reformation tension this was a totally revolutionary approach, but most effective. Francis said, "One can catch more flies with a spoonful of honey than with a hundred barrels of vinegar". Through his gentleness he won people to the truth. Of course in today's ecumenical climate our mission is not to win converts from other churches, but to win the unchurched and those alienated from the Church. This will be achieved by gentleness, rather than by confrontation.

Pope Francis understands this well. He knows that the Church is often regarded as out of date and irrelevant to the aspirations of a secular society.

At a recent priest's charismatic retreat in Rome he was asked how we can communicate the truth of the gospel in the face of an aggressively secular agenda. How do we meet this situation where there is so much opposition or indifference to the Christian message? His answer was to avoid trying to convince solely by disputation, but to win others by the way we live. Just as in the early Church where their lives were so radically different, and their love for others, especially for the poor, was so attractive, we need the same witness today. The Pope told the priests to live the beatitudes and win the world by the quality of their lives. The gospel genuinely lived is very attractive indeed.

But is the gospel being lived? The much quoted comment of G.K. Chesterton still applies, "The Christian ideal has not been tried and found wanting; it has been found difficult and left untried". At this time in history our greatest challenge is not to find strategies for evangelisation and clever programs to bring people back to the faith. Rather it is for all Christians to live the gospel uncompromisingly and witness to the presence of Christ in our communities by our love for one another and for the poorest of the poor. The unbeliever will be touched when he or she encounters the tenderness and gentle love of Christ in the way we live together, and in the way we relate to others, and welcome them into our lives.

## The Meekest Man on Earth

As we seek to grow in gentleness we are confronted with the problem of anger. We are told by God in Exodus that Moses was "the meekest man on earth" (Numb 12:3). However, he was not always like that. He had been left as a baby in the bulrushes when Pharaoh was killing all first-born Israelites. Found by Pharaoh's daughter, who took pity on this abandoned child, he was brought up as a prince in the royal household. As a young man Moses was shocked by the cruel, oppressive way his people were enslaved. This affected him deeply. One day he saw an Egyptian unjustly strike a Hebrew. He was so enraged by this injustice that in retaliation he killed the Egyptian on the spot. When the murder came to light he escaped to Midian and spent years in the wilderness tending sheep. No doubt this was a time for him to confront the darkness within his heart.

Then one day he saw a bush being consumed by fire but with no apparent cause (Ex 3:1-6). This intrigued him. As he approached, he heard the voice "Come no nearer. Take off your shoes for you are on holy ground. I am the God of your father, the God of Abraham, Isaac and Jacob." To take off his shoes was to yield control to God, to give over himself to the Almighty, recognizing his weakness, but acknowledging God's strength. This was Moses' moment of transformation. The long hours in solitude had prepared him for this encounter. In meeting the living God he recognised more clearly the arrogance of his youth. He was able to relinquish his need to take things into his own hands, and yield rather to the hand of God. From this encounter Moses was now commissioned by God to lead his people out of slavery in Egypt, by confronting Pharaoh and demanding their release and the freedom to leave the country. God could now use Moses as the leader of his people because he had come to realize his nothingness. No longer would Moses seek to control things his way, but he would do things God's way. This is gentleness.

Later when the Israelites were in the desert Moses' gentleness was put to the test (Numb 12:1-16). Miriam and Aaron had spoken against Moses because he had taken a Cushite for his wife. But Moses did not defend himself. He suffered their taunts without retaliating. He waited for God to vindicate him. And it surely happened. Miriam was struck with leprosy because she had spoken against God's anointed one. But then, instead of gloating over this misfortune, Moses pleaded with God to heal her. And the Lord answered his prayer.

## Anger: Good and Bad

We need to note that while Moses was "the most gentle man on the earth" he was also a strong leader of his people. He was no soft-belly weakling. This was even more true of Jesus. The gooey sentimental image sometimes given of a "meek and mild" Jesus of whom butter would not melt in his mouth, is a travesty of the truth. An emasculated Jesus is not very attractive at all. The popular image of Jesus as soft, sentimental, and super sensitive, never challenging, but always seeking to make people feel good, is not true to the gospels. He angrily took up a whip and drove out the money changers from the Temple because they were misusing the house of God. But notice his gentleness towards the poor who were selling turtle doves and pigeons. He kindly asked them to move on (Jn 2:16).

Anger of itself is a normal human emotion. When Jesus saw a man with a withered hand on the fringes of the people in the synagogue because he was deformed, he called him out into the middle. He challenged the synagogue officials whether it is against the law to heal on the Sabbath day. They were silent. Mark says, "grieved to find them so obstinate, he *looked angrily round at them*, and said to the man 'stretch out your hand'." As he did so the man was healed (Mk 3:2-5).

With Jesus anger was always righteous. With us it rarely is. We need to learn to control our anger and use it constructively in service of the Lord and of others. People have different ways of dealing with their anger. Often these ways are ineffective and destructive. When things happen that annoy them, or an injustice is done against them, people often don't know how to express their anger helpfully. They burst out in uncontrolled rage. This sort of hot anger is destructive, since they pour out their rage upon another, and do more damage. Others do the exact opposite with their anger. Their sense of decency doesn't allow them to rage so they turn the anger in upon themselves in an orgy of self-hate, or they repress the anger, relegating it to the semi-conscious, pretending it is not there. These are people who are too passive in their response, possibly afraid of their emotions or maybe governed by mistaken moral norms, which don't allow them to express their anger creatively.

People who repress anger are like a walking time bomb, or to use another image, they have a volcano within them ready to explode unexpectedly. Actually some of the nicest people I have met have been carrying repressed anger. They have spent their lives being very nice to everyone, but have never confronted situations in which they needed to stand up for their rights or needed simply to speak the truth in love. They are like the man who came home one day and found a tiger in the house. Using a chair he managed to force the tiger into the basement. He slammed the door on the basement and then went about things as if all was well. But he still had this wild tiger underneath. When friends came over they could hear the noise below. They sensed something was wrong. What does the man do? He is in big trouble. Some people are like this, and the repressed tiger is ready to roar.

## Strength Under Control

We need to bring our aggressive instincts under control. This is particularly an issue for men. Alcohol fuelled violence amongst young men has become a major social issue. But while men are more prone to physical violence, whether it is in the home or on the street, women struggle with anger also. They may occasionally attack physically, but more often they will lash out with the caustic tongue that cuts more deeply than a dagger. Gentleness is "strength under control". A wild stallion running free on the range is full of aggressive energy. When it is lassoed and brought into the corral it snorts and rears up uncontrollably. The horse-tamer ventures into the corral to win the animal over with gentleness. He whispers gently to the horse seeking to win its trust. At first the horse reacts angrily, resisting all attempts to subdue it. But then gradually after some time the horse begins to settle and allows the trainer to come close. After much gentle persuasion, whispering in the ear of the horse, the trainer is able to put on the bridle and bit, and then the saddle. Now all the untamed energy can be channelled and used constructively under the hand of the master. Jesus is our "horse-whisperer". He wants to bring out innate strength under control. We learn to trust him, and to accept his will in our daily lives without anger or rebellion. We become joyfully yoked to doing his will. Our aggressive energies become tamed and channelled by God.

Sadly in today's society aggressive, overbearing, manipulative behaviour has become fashionable in political and activist movements. This can carry over into personal relationships as well. It seems fair game to be overly aggressive to get what you want. It is a sort of "jungle mentality" under the rule of "survival of the fittest" and the fear that "nice guys finish last". This is a general attitude towards life, and to others, that fails to recognise the dignity of the other. There is no love, but rather an attempt to get what you want by whatever means you can, while keeping within societal rules. People may not be classified as overt bullies, but they can still fail to relate respectfully. By force of personality, or strong opinionated language, or emotional manipulation, or trying to win the argument by attacking the character of the person, many are failing to meet one another with respect and reverence for the dignity of the other person. The truly gentle person is genuinely assertive, not afraid to speak the truth in love, nor to act in unpopular ways that confront people with the truth, but never in a deliberately combative or offensive manner. The way of Jesus is neither timid and self-demeaning nor is it overly aggressive. It is the way of love.

## Francis de Sales: peace of soul

The spiritual tradition of the church attests to the importance of not letting our emotions become our masters, but rather making them our servants. Francis de Sales, following Augustine, counsels not to let anger grow within the soul, even when we feel justified to be angry.[10] He advises to "nip it in the bud" before it takes hold as a bitter root within us. When the apostles on the Sea of Galilee were in a storm beyond their control, and they thought they were sinking, they cried for help. Jesus stood up in the boat and commanded the wind and the waves to be still. Likewise, if we call on him when anger arises and storms within us, Jesus will restore peace to the soul.

As Paul says, "never let the sun go down on your anger" (Eph 4:26). In other words, deal with it now, rather than allow it to consume us with its wrath. If there is a need to be reconciled with someone, go to the person as soon as you have cooled down, repair the fault with forgiveness and relate towards the person in a spirit of gentleness. When we move in the opposite spirit to the demands of the irrational emotion, it comes into order and its energies can be used appropriately. Francis urges us that when we are in a time of tranquillity always practice gentleness of speech and manner, so it becomes our habitual way of being.

Francis de Sales also insists on learning to be gentle on ourselves.[11] Many suffer from self-hate, or endless recriminations against themselves. When we fail and sin, we have a tendency to catastrophize and think "I am a failure", "I am hopeless", "I have no future". We whip ourselves into a frenzy of self-condemnation, and fall into a pit of despondency or even despair. He counsels us to be displeased with our sins, but not to wreak havoc on ourselves. "We correct ourselves much better by a calm and steady repentance than by that which is harsh, turbulent, and passionate." Just as a loving father gains the best from a child by a gentle, affectionate reproof, so God our Father would also. Rage and passion never helped anyone to change. He tells us, "Raise up your heart again whenever it falls, but meekly, humbling yourself before God…detest the sin that has been committed… and with great courage and confidence in his mercy return to the way of virtue, which you had forsaken."

## Don Bosco: Win the Young by Gentleness

Gentleness is a fruit of the Spirit, and is essential for any parent or figure in authority. It mirrors the heart of God. Many suffer deep wounds due to experiences of rejection or angry abusive behaviour from parents. Consequently, they tend to think of God as vindictive and punishing, a harsh taskmaster who cannot be trusted. When forming young people we need to win them over gently by love and pray with them for the healing of the heart that has been bruised by the misuse of authority. Gradually the heart begins to trust again and find restoration in the loving arms of our Father God. St John Bosco, a priest in nineteenth century Turin, commonly known as Don Bosco, was in touch with this dynamic. At that time Turin was teeming with young lads, poor, often orphaned, unemployed and inclined to mischief. Don Bosco gathered them by the attraction of gentleness and inspired them to grow in virtue.

When he was a nine-year-old boy John Bosco dreamt that he was standing in a field, surrounded by a crowd of other young boys who were playing and shouting, full of energy and fun.[12] Then he saw another group of boys fighting each other, yelling and cursing the whole time. He immediately charged into this group, shouting for them to stop. They ignored him. Frustrated he began to beat all of them, trying to force them to obey him. Naturally, all the boys turned on him and laid into him. Suddenly a tall man dressed in shining white came towards them. Everyone stopped. "You'll never help these boys by beating them," he said. "Be kind and gentle. Lead them and teach them how evil sin is and how desirable virtue is. Then they will become your friends." Then the man disappeared. The boys around him then changed into a pack of wolves, growling and snapping at one another. Then a woman appeared, dressed in a glittering golden cloak. She took John's hand and told him not to be afraid. She said gently, "What I am about to do for these animals you will do for all my children." Immediately the wolves turned into lambs, bleating and playing joyfully. The boy did not understand what the lady meant. Only years later did Don Bosco realize the prophetic nature of the dream. It described his life's mission.

After being ordained a priest in 1841 Bosco moved to Turin. One day when he heard a commotion in the sacristy he investigated to find the old sacristan raining down blows upon a young lad. When Bosco came on the scene the boy took the opportunity to flee. The priest demanded that the sacristan go and fetch the boy. "Why?" asked the sacristan. "Because any boy in trouble is my friend" said Don Bosco. Through gentleness and kindness he quickly won the boy over and invited him to come to catechism class even though he could not read or write. Soon others came and before long there was quite a crowd for the young priest to handle. This was the beginning of a life-long ministry.

In an age when teaching was guided by the principle of "spare the rod, spoil the child", Don Bosco brought a revolution of love. He once told a friend, "Friendship breeds affection and affection breeds confidence. It opens the heart, and young people approach their teachers, assistants and superiors without fear." He called the religious congregation, which sprung up from some of his more dedicated boys, the Salesians, after St Francis de Sales. It was all about gentleness. The dream he had as a young boy came true. With the presence of Jesus and Our Lady he met the boys with gentleness and won them over. They were no longer like wild wolves but gentle as lambs. In one of his letters to his brothers he wrote, "It is much easier to get angry than to be patient, to threaten a boy rather than persuade him. I would even say that usually it is so much more convenient for our own impatience and pride to punish them than to correct them patiently with firmness and gentleness."[13] He knew from long experience that angry outbursts, looks of contempt and a tirades of hurtful words never help the soul to change, but only build fear, lack of self-confidence, and a heart full of hurt and resentment.

The meek are those who have the Lord's heart to humbly serve the other. At times they may not feel like serving, nor even enjoy serving, but they humble themselves with "towel and water" like Jesus. They treat all whom they meet with respect and honour, not only the highly placed and eminent, but also and especially the lowly and underprivileged, those without worldly honours. They have a deep respect for others, and a compassion for the wounds in their hearts, winning them with the persuasion of love, and empowering them to be who God has called them to be.

# 3
# BLESSED ARE THOSE WHO MOURN

*Blessed are those who mourn, for they will be comforted Mt 5:5*

## Tears of Sorrow; Redeeming Grief

At first glance there seems nothing blessed about mourning. We have all experienced deep sorrow at some time in our lives and remember it as a time of affliction, anguish and abandonment. This could tempt us to think Jesus is using symbolic language and did not mean the heart-wrenching experience of real mourning. But the Greek word used here connotes intense grief, a harrowing of the heart which leads to bitter tears. How can this be blessed? Commentators and spiritual writers reflecting on this beatitude offer a number of applications.

Maybe the most popular contemporary interpretation is the hidden blessing found in the unexpected loss of a loved one. This is probably not the original biblical meaning, but is still a worthwhile perspective. After all Jesus himself wept over the death of Lazarus, his friend (Jn11:35). Those present remarked, "See how much he loved him". Jesus was no doubt moved by the tears of Mary who had thrown herself at his feet protesting that Lazarus would not have died if Jesus had been with them. But when he had heard that Lazarus was dying Jesus had deliberately delayed coming. Why? In the mystery of God's ways through the death of Lazarus Jesus gives us a sign of resurrection. When he tells them to roll the stone away from the entrance to the tomb, Martha protests, "Lord, by now he will smell; this is the fourth day". After so long the body would already be decaying. Jesus replied, "Have I not told you that if you believe you will see the glory of God?". Then lifting up his eyes to heaven he prays, and then cries out, "Lazarus, come out!" And Lazarus emerged from the tomb to the amazement of all.

This beautiful story is for our encouragement in times of grief and loss; times when our hearts are shattered and so full of anguish that we feel we could never be restored. The presence of Jesus with us brings great consolation, and assurance that death does not have the last say. Those who die in Christ will rise again. He weeps with us when we weep, and his presence makes our sorrow bearable, offering us a light in the darkness which otherwise threatens to swallow us up. Notice that Jesus says, "If you believe you will see the glory of God". The blessing presumes faith.

Not all who mourn loss in their lives will be blessed; from experience we know that unfortunately many through lack of faith fall into despair. They cannot take hold of the blessing available for them. They feel there is no hope. Paul says, "We do not want you to be ignorant, brothers, about those who have died, so that you may not grieve as others do who have no hope" (1 Thess 4:13). Sobbing profusely at the loss of a loved one is a real human experience, not to be suppressed, but by the grace of God, and our faith in Christ, we do not despair. There is a joy deeper than sorrow which comes from the knowledge of God's unconditional love. We are told that Jesus "was sorrowful to the point of death" in Gethsemane, but he was sustained by "the joy that was set before him" (Heb 12:2). In our sorrow as we join with him in his suffering we share in the hope that springs eternal. This is a foretaste of the future joy when "He will wipe away every tear from their eyes, and death shall be no more, neither shall there be mourning nor crying nor pain anymore" (Rev 21:4).

## Consolation in Suffering

The beatitude is not only for those mourning the death of loved ones, but also for those mourning the loss of things, places, times, abilities, hopes, dreams, and many good things of this world that are taken from us unexpectedly. We mourn for loss of health, loss of friendships, loss of property through floods or bushfires, loss of a career opportunity, and so on. Our pilgrim journey on this earth is punctuated with grief after grief. A rather joyful priest friend of mine, returning from his parish visitation, used to sigh, "valley of tears and world of sorrows!" The heavy burdens many carry seem unbearable. But this beatitude assures us that whatever the tragedy or calamity that visits us, God's blessing is hidden within it. We need to ask, "Where is God in all this?" Catherine of Siena used to liken these agonising experiences to an orange: "Under the bitter rind one finds a hidden sweetness". The consolation of God is assured to those of faith who turn to him in their sorrow. In their worst times they are aware that Jesus suffered with us, and he continues to be with us in our suffering now. He is in the garden of Gethsemane with us, his heart torn open and weeping bitter tears, but surrendering to the mysterious will of the Father. With him we have the confidence to yield to the will of God and to place all our trust in him.

This beatitude also applies to all who "weep with those who weep" (Rom 12:15). The consolation we receive from God in our lives builds in us a compassion for others. It connects with the later beatitude, "Blessed are the merciful". Paul tells us "we have a gentle Father, the God of all consolation, who comforts us in all our sorrows, so that we can offer others, in their sorrows, the consolation that we have received from God ourselves" (2Cor 1: 3-4). We are to have hearts like Jesus when he encountered the widow of Nain weeping for her only son as he was being carried out for burial. We are told Jesus was deeply moved, sharing in her grief, a sadness that led him to act with mercy. Touching the bier he commanded, "Young man, rise up!" The man rose up from the dead and Jesus gave him to his mother. In the ministry of consolation we feel the Lord's heart for those grieving, whatever their loss. We are to be the Lord's lips, his eyes, his touch, his words. At the Second Vatican Council the fathers of the Church expressed it poignantly: "The joys and the hopes, the griefs and anxieties of the men and women of this age, especially those who are poor or in any way afflicted, these are the joys and hopes, the griefs and anxieties of the followers of Christ. Indeed, nothing genuinely human fails to raise an echo in their hearts."[14]

## Sorrow for Sins

We can also apply this beatitude to the grace of repentance. Blessed are those who weep for their sins. The Holy Spirit convicts us of sin. It is a wonderful grace from God when we can acknowledge honestly the sinfulness of our hearts, not excusing ourselves or rationalizing or blaming others for our faults. Under God's grace we have revealed to us the truth that sets us free. The Lord calls us to conversion, "return to me with all your heart, fasting, weeping, and mourning; rend your hearts and turn to the Lord your God again, for he is gracious and merciful" (Joel 2:12-13). By the grace of compunction we weep interiorly and maybe also shed tears outwardly. Before the Cross of Jesus we realize that it was our sins that nailed him there, but it was his loving mercy that kept him there. Our tears are not only because of our shame and guilt, but also for love of him who died for us. We are filled with gratitude for his saving love. But we do not weep with despair.

Paul tells us there are two ways of being sorrowful for our sins (2 Cor 8-10). One way is godly and brings the blessing; recognising our guilt we turn to the Lord confident in his mercy. The other way is ungodly, since it is full of self-pity and useless remorse, which turns one inwards in self-condemning thoughts, and leads to despair. We can become victims of self-hate and paralysed by a self-defeating emotions. Having come to see the reality of our sin, we must certainly mourn for our miserably broken state. But the grace given by God is to make a decision not to fall into despair; rather to trust in the salvation he has won for us, to believe in his forgiveness. It is simply a matter of confessing our sin and letting God lift us up again. This is the difference between Peter and Judas. Both betrayed the Lord on the same night. Judas had led the enemies of Jesus to the Garden; Peter had denied that he even knew the Lord. Both had sinned grievously. Judas allowed Satan to enter him and did not turn to the Lord for forgiveness. He shut himself out from the mercy of Jesus. But Peter at his lowest moment encountered the merciful eyes of Jesus. He did not avoid this gaze, but in that moment realized the perversity of his heart and his utter lostness without God. He went outside and wept bitterly, but not in despair. He put his trust in the mercy of God. Blessed are those who mourn like Peter.

The blessedness in being filled with sorrow for our sins is the accompanying joy of repentance. We share in the joy of God himself. When the lost sheep is found by the good shepherd, or the lost coin recovered by the house-wife there is great rejoicing. And when the father welcomes home the son who had been lost he rejoices by killing the fatted calf and calls the whole household to share his joy. Jesus said, "There is more rejoicing in heaven over one repentant sinner than over ninety-nine who have no need of repentance" (Lk15:7). The joy of being free of the shame and guilt attached to our sin, the joy of being again in the father's arms, the joy of "breathing again" the life of the Spirit, the joy of receiving mercy which we do not deserve, all of this and more is the blessedness of those who weep for their sins.

## Weeping Over the World

Jesus was probably speaking primarily about another kind of grieving; a weeping over the world and the manifold trouble that besets humanity. Blessed are they who grieve for the terrible suffering in the world, much of which is caused by human negligence, arrogance and sin. This involves being in touch with the heart of Jesus for the world. We are told that "when he saw the crowds he felt sorry for them because they were harassed and dejected like sheep without a shepherd" (Mt 9: 36). The word used in the Greek for "felt sorry" means much more than a sentimental emotion or a twinge of sympathy; rather it means he was "wrenched in his guts", moved deeply in the depths of his heart, mourning over them because they had not yet had the opportunity to respond to the word of salvation. Their situation was desperate because they were part of a culture and a social system which held them oppressed and without consolation or hope. This insight into the heart of Jesus is revealing for us; under God's grace we will share the same heart of compassion for our contemporaries.

In Luke's gospel it is recorded that twice Jesus wept over Jerusalem. In the first instance he laments, "Jerusalem, Jerusalem, you that kill the prophets and stone those who are sent to you! How often have I longed to gather you to myself, as a hen gathers her brood under her wings, but you were not willing!" (Lk13: 34-35) The love in the heart of Jesus for his own people, just like a mother hen wanting to bring her chicks under her wings, is the love he has for all human beings for whom he died. The second lamentation over Jerusalem was just before Jesus entered the city: "As he drew near and came in sight of the city he shed tears over it and said, "If you in your turn had only understood on this day the message of peace! But, alas it is hidden from your eyes!" (Lk 19:41-42). Jesus grieves over the obstinacy of those who refuse to accept the good news and do not take the opportunity of this time of mercy. We too weep over the cities of this world where the distress of people is so heavy a burden. We feel the pain of the widespread rejection of Jesus, but this stirs us to greater love. We grow in the gift of intercession, holding in our hearts people captive to sin, and oppressed by their situation.

## Standing for Others before God

In November 1938, when Hiltler ordered the Synagogues and Jewish properties in Germany to be vandalized, he launched a concerted campaign to annihilate the Jewish people. A forty- nine- year old Carmelite nun knew that her life's work was at hand. Sr. Benedicta of the Cross, previously known as Edith Stein, could sense that it would not be long before she would be called to make the ultimate sacrifice for her people. Edith had grown up in a Jewish family, but in her early years had lost the faith.[15] Yet as a young woman she had a deep thirst for truth. Placing herself under Edmund Husserl, she became an acclaimed professional philosopher. At the age of 26 she providentially attended a Christian funeral of a friend of Husserl. She was puzzled by the Christian faith and serenity of the widow who was mourning her husband. When she enquired about her peaceful state the widow simply replied, "I accept my loss as my part in the Cross of Christ which brings healing and life to all". The witness of this woman's faith rocked the sophistication of Edith's philosophy. A couple of years later Edith was left alone in a friend's house. A little bored she picked up the life of Teresa of Avila. It was compelling reading. By the time morning came she knew she had finally found the truth. To the chagrin of her mother and family she became baptised into the Catholic Church. Some years later she took vows as a Carmelite nun.

Edith understood that her offering of herself to the Lord in Carmel was in a mysterious way for the sake of her Jewish people. She identified with Queen Esther in the Old Testament when the Jewish people were in Exile.[16] Esther had become queen by the choice of king Ahasuerus, who did not know that she was actually a Jewish woman. Haman, the king's chancellor hated the Jewish people and by deception had the king sign a royal decree for the extermination of the Jews. Queen Esther was prevailed upon by a leader of the Jewish people to plead on their behalf before the king. But this meant taking her own life in her hands since to appear before the king without a summons meant instant death. To save her people Esther prayed earnestly to God to protect her from the king's rage and to change the heart of the king.

The prayer of Esther became the prayer of Edith who was in a similar situation. Edith saw herself as "taken from among her people precisely that she might stand for them before the King". Her vocation in Carmel was to stand before the living God, the King of Kings, and to focus her prayer for the sufferings of her people. She embraced the Cross for the sake of her people, not only that they be protected from persecution, but also that they may come to know their Saviour, Jesus Christ. She felt deeply the sorrowful predicament of her people, being one with them in their affliction. Like Esther she carried her people in her heart, ready to stand *with* them in all their anxieties, and to stand *for* them before God. She offered her life for her people.

She had been transferred to Holland for safety, but when the Dutch bishops publicly denounced the Nazi regime, all those of Jewish descent in monasteries and convents were rounded up and transported in cattle trucks to concentration camps. Edith and her sister Rosa were arrested and forcibly thrown into a rail truck with the others. She willingly offered herself as a holocaust on the altar of sacrifice for her own.

A Dutch employee at the camp remembered Edith as full of peace, walking amongst the other prisoners, talking with them and praying with them. Incensed at the cruel treatment she was receiving he offered to contact Dutch authorities and attempt to arrange her freedom. In his eyes she was no longer a Jew. But Edith responded, "No, no, don't please…If I were exempted from the fate of the others, my life would be destroyed forever". She knew this was her highest hour, the fulfilment of her sacrifice. Soon afterwards she was gassed to death. Blessed are they who mourn, they shall be consoled. Edith's mourning for the Jewish people was not narrowly focussed. Because she was united with the Cross of Jesus she shared in his suffering for all, the man of sorrows, acquainted with grief, his universal love for all men and women.

## Crying out for Mercy on our World

Blessed are those who mourn over the world today, they shall be comforted. We join with so many of our contemporaries in today's situation to weep for the tragedies of our age. Foremost in our minds would be the horrific manifestations of evil perpetrated by the so-called Islamic State, the unpredictable outbreaks of terrorism, the mass movement of refugees due to war in the Middle East, the numerous conflicts in different countries, the inequality in distribution of wealth, the failure to overcome world hunger, the proliferation of addictive drugs, human trafficking, the confusion in human sexuality and loss of family life, the legitimation of abortion and euthanasia, and numerous social problems too many to mention. God's faithful ones under the sign of the Cross are the ones "who sigh and groan over all the abominations that are committed in the city" (Ez 9:4). They know that this world with all its sorrows is not our lasting dwelling place. While being strangers in this world they are also committed to changing the world for good. In their grief they enter into intercession, crying out to God for his mercy upon all humanity, which is suffering so profoundly.

In this spirit of weeping for the world Pope John Paul II dedicated humanity to the mercy of God. On 17$^{th}$ August 2002 at a Mass for the dedication of the Divine Mercy shrine in Lagiewniki Poland he said:

> How greatly today's world needs God's mercy! In every continent, from

the depth of human suffering, a cry of mercy seems to rise up. Where hatred and the thirst for revenge dominate, where war brings suffering and death to the innocent, there the grace of mercy is needed in order to settle human minds and hearts and to bring about peace.....

Today, therefore, in this Shrine, I wish solemnly to entrust the world to Divine Mercy. I do so with the burning desire that the message of God's merciful love, proclaimed here through Saint Faustina, may be made known to all the peoples of the earth and fill their hearts with hope.[17]

# Lamenting Unbelief

In the Psalms we hear a lament that is oddly very contemporary. The psalmist cries, "My tears have become my bread, by night, by day, as I hear it said all day long: 'Where is your God?'" (Ps 42:4) We find ourselves frustrated and weeping helplessly over the new surge of philosophical atheism which relies upon the so-called certitudes of science to interpret reality. The psalmist mourns, "With cries that pierce me to the heart, my enemies revile me, saying to me all the day long: 'Where is your God?'" We share in the weakness of God who is silent before this affront to his majesty. "God's weakness is stronger than human strength" (1Cor 1:25). This phenomenon of hostile rejection of God may infuriate us at times, but when we are truly moving in the Spirit it should evoke in us a deep compassion for unbelievers. Mother Teresa, who knew poverty like few others, once made the observation that the greatest poverty of all is with those who think they can do without God. They are to be pitied the most, not in a condescending way, but with the same heart as Jesus when he wept over Jerusalem. The greatest loss a human being can endure is the loss of God.

Sadly with the militant atheists of our day, who regard religion to be the greatest problem in the universe, we see the extreme arrogance of hearts hardened against God. But it is good to remember the insight of Shakespeare: "the one who protests too much" may not be as far from the truth as we imagine. Those who are fighting against the faith may very well be more open than those who are completely apathetic and indifferent. Yet it surely breaks the heart of God to see such animosity towards him, and such ridicule towards his saving death on the Cross. And how it breaks our hearts also; not leading to despair, but spurring us on to find new ways in the Spirit to bring the good news of Jesus.

Those who mourn will be comforted. The prophet Isaiah, speaking of the joy and hope of the people of Israel who will return from seventy years of exile in Babylon, proclaimed words appropriate for us today: "'Console my people, console them' says your God. Speak to the heart of Jerusalem and call to her that her time of service is ended, that her sin is atoned for" (Is 40: 1). God was bringing his exiles home and restoring them to their worship and their land. He had heard their cry as they wept by the rivers of Babylon, longing for their homeland. This was the time that God had come "to comfort all those who mourn, to strengthen those who mourn Zion by giving them a garland, instead of ashes, oil of gladness for mourning, a garment of praise instead of discouragement." (Is 61:3). They had been through the furnace of suffering and now joy and liberation was to come.

Our present situation in today's world will engage us in much suffering with the people of our time. We enter into solidarity with the suffering of our age and do not seek to escape from it. Our attitude is not just one of sympathising with others, but of actually sharing in their pain. We feel the heart of God for our contemporaries. Although God does not suffer in himself, because he is God, he *suffers with* humanity. This is the reality of Jesus crucified. God the father was not indifferent to the suffering of his Son. Rather he suffered *with* Jesus. "If God did not spare his only Son, but gave him up for us; after such a gift would he withhold anything from us?" (Rom 8:32). We can be confident that no matter how dire the situation is in the world today that God is always drawing near, sharing in the pain, and giving the wisdom to know what to do, and the grace to endure our plight with hope-filled hearts. On the Cross Jesus entered into solidarity with the worst of human misery, whether inflicted by violent atrocities or natural calamities. And the Father suffered with him. No matter how rotten the human situation becomes, our hope is founded in the sure knowledge that God the Father raised Jesus from the dead. This is our joy which no one can take from us. This is the joy we proclaim to the world.

## Woe to You Who Laugh

Luke's version of this beatitude is characteristically direct and confronting. "Blessed are you who weep now; you shall laugh…Woe to you who laugh now; you shall mourn and weep". The contrast is between weeping and laughing. To understand what Jesus is saying we need to ask what he means in each instance by laughing and weeping. His warning to those who laugh now is not a ban on laughter. Unfortunately, one strain of the spiritual tradition interpreted it this way. This led to a joyless asceticism not in imitation of Jesus but in service of a negative spirituality, which lost a sense of the best of what it means to be human. We do not have any explicit scriptural text about Jesus laughing, but it is hard to imagine the Lord never cracking a smile with his disciples or heartily laughing with his friends and those with whom he dined.

When he says "woe to you who laugh" he is addressing those who indulge in illicit pleasure, warning that the thrill will pass and they will be left with interior emptiness. Sensate pleasure and self-indulgence cannot provide lasting joy. It fails to produce what it promises. There may be lots of laughter but it is superficial and frivolous, covering over the emptiness in the soul. It is not true joy. The irrepressible desire in us for true joy is not meant to be directed exclusively to earthly things, as if they can ultimately satisfy us. Rather, only God can bring us the joy we desire. If we fall into the trap of seeking to be satisfied by earthly pleasures or achievements we will be eternally frustrated, unable to fulfil our lives in the way intended by God. This is the nature of hell. When the pursuit of pleasure rebels against God's law then God permits pain and death to follow.

Jesus promised joy to his disciples, but it would be a joy born through suffering. Those who try to set up a painless existence, selfishly grabbing for what this life can offer, will miss this joy. At the Last Supper Jesus told his disciples, "I tell you most solemnly, you will be weeping and wailing while the world will rejoice; you will be sorrowful, but your sorrow will turn to joy". He likens his coming death and resurrection to the suffering and travail experienced by a woman in child-birth. When the child is born she forgets the pain and is full of joy as she embraces her baby. "So it is with you" says Jesus, "you are sad now, but I shall see you again, and your hearts will be full of joy, and that joy no one shall take from you" (Jn 16: 20-22). Lasting joy, which comes from the heart of Jesus, does not come cheaply through a few jokes and empty laughter. Rather joy comes out of suffering. As for Jesus, so for us: "for the joy that was set before him Jesus endured the Cross" (Heb 12:2).

This beatitude reminds us of the emptiness and banality of much laughter that goes on in response to crude comedy and television shows which are full of vulgarity and spiteful satire, using lewd jokes and ridiculing others. This is the sort of laughter about which Jesus warns us. An even more pernicious "laughter" is an attitude of the elite, opulent and privileged ones, who can afford to fill their lives with endless pleasure and entertainment, and ignore the plight of the poor and marginalised. Endless frivolity without any insight into the reason we are on this planet, and without any genuine love of others, is a fruitless existence. This would be a wasted life. Anyone who journeys through life without having genuinely loved is a walking tragedy. To discover love is to embrace pain. It is to enter into self-sacrifice for the sake of others. It is to die with Jesus, so that we may know the joy of his resurrection.

## The Witness of Joy

Addiction to pleasant sensations, whether they be physical, emotional or spiritual, will never lead us to God. Jesus calls us to detachment of heart which we considered with the first beatitude. Only in this way can we be spiritually free to be able to love and hence be truly happy. Joy is the true note of the Christian. The world wants to paint us as killjoys; supposedly taking the fun out of life. Rather, Jesus invites us to true joy, genuine happiness. The worldly mentality fosters the illusion that more fun, more entertainment, more adventures in themselves will make you happy. Unfortunately, worldly people so often have an empty hole in the heart, like that of a donut, which just cannot be filled, no matter how many pleasurable pursuits they undertake. But followers of Jesus have found that the true joy is found in God's immense love for each one of us, and until we discover this joy our hearts are not fulfilled. The Christian knows that "the joy of the Lord is our strength" (Neh 8:10). Once we find the joy of the Lord we then find in a new way the beauty of his creation and the wonderful gifts he has lavished upon us. But we don't fall upon these beautiful things of his creation as if they alone will satisfy. We enjoy them, but hold on to them lightly, since our ultimate joy is in union with God alone.

A joyless Christian is a walking contradiction. But unfortunately there are still some around. Friedrich Nietzsche, the father of modern atheism, once made the comment about the Christians of his day: "They say they are redeemed, but they sure don't look like it". He could not see the joy which they proclaimed to have. That is Christianity gone wrong. Our joy is grounded in knowing we are redeemed by Christ, and we want to witness his love to the world. Laughter is still "the best medicine". It only becomes a selfish reality when it becomes an idol, claiming to be the dominant source of life, even at the expense of other's suffering. We need to laugh and to relax and have fun together. This experience is qualitatively different when celebrated in Christ, rather than degenerating into foolishly crass amusement which is not giving glory to God. As Paul urges, "Rejoice in the Lord always; again I say rejoice" (Phil 3:4).

# 4
# BLESSED ARE THOSE WHO HUNGER AND THIRST FOR RIGHTEOUSNESS

*Blessed are those who hunger and thirst for righteousness, for they will be filled* Mt 5:6

Those who hunger and thirst for righteousness tap into the deep longing in every human heart for more; for something greater than we presently experience. It is the hunger and thirst for Christ himself. It stirs in us a holy discontent with things as they are, and a restlessness of heart towards something greater, leading to truth, love and God himself. This thirst for God opens us to his kingdom. When the Holy Spirit is released within us, this fundamental thirst, which is naturally within every human being, is transformed into a quest for holiness, for union with God, and a burning desire to do his will.

## The Righteous One

Matthew's understanding of righteousness is close to what we would call goodness or holiness. The righteous person is someone who is notable for their virtue, someone who thinks and acts in the way Jesus does. When Joseph, who was betrothed to Mary, discovered she was pregnant, even though they were not yet formally married, he chose not to publicly expose her and potentially embarrass her. Instead he took the legitimate option of breaking the bond privately. Matthew tells us Joseph did this because he was a "righteous man" (Mt 1:19). Some translations say he was a "man of honour" or a "just" man. The sense is a man who is morally upright, having the heart of God. The righteous person's behaviour is characteristically morally impeccable, trusting of God, and acting according to his ways. John the Baptist is said to have come as "a pattern of true righteousness" but the Pharisees did not believe him, while tax collectors and prostitutes did (Mt 21:32). Jesus reproached the Pharisees because on the outside they appeared to be righteous, but on the inside they were "full of hypocrisy and wickedness" (Mt 23:28-29). They were all show. The Greek word (*hupokrites*) from which the English word hypocrite is derived is taken from the theatre. It means acting out a role which is not really you. This sort of false religious behaviour drew Jesus' sharpest rebukes. He called them "white-washed sepulchres". On the outside they were lily white but inside corrupt to the core.

Jesus said "If your righteousness goes no deeper than that of the Scribes and Pharisees you cannot enter the kingdom of God" (Mt 5:20). So it is a matter of the heart first. A change of heart is needed more than anything else. Jesus saw injustices all around him but he did not launch any program of political or social reform. While his preaching was mainly with the poor, broken and disenfranchised, his words were directed primarily towards conversion, a change of heart. He did not rally them to some activist campaign to attain their basic human rights. He knew that only a profound, radical change of heart and soul in one individual after another would ultimately bring about the change of a corrupt social system. If we don't have righteousness within us we will never be able to bring it to the world outside of us.

## A New Heart

A true story I have told elsewhere comes to mind.[18] In 1989 Stoffel van den Berg, a wealthy banker, was entering South African politics to defend the policy of apartheid which was now seriously under question. He had grown up believing that black people were inferior and not worthy of having the same privileges as the whites. His first speech of his campaign ended with these words, "I'll go to my grave knowing that apartheid must be right, for blacks as well as for whites." He received a standing ovation. But all this changed soon afterwards. When trying to overcome a lorry on a narrow road he miscalculated and had a head-on collision with an on-coming car. The moment before the crash he saw the terrified face of the other driver. That was the last thing he remembered until he regained consciousness in hospital five weeks later. The surgeon was at his bedside and told him he was lucky to be alive. He explained to Stoffel that the other driver had died, and only moments later Stoffel's heart had stopped. But they were able to give him a donor heart that was immediately available. Stoffell exclaimed, "Not the driver of the other car?" The surgeon nodded. "But ...wasn't he black?" asked Stoffel in disbelief. "Yes, he was," said the surgeon. "And it may come as a surprise to you Mr van den Berg, your body doesn't realize that."

The surgeon then explained to Stoffel that despite the success of the transplant his other injuries were so severe that he would probably only live another four years. After six weeks recuperation Stoffel returned home, gave up his career at the bank, took out his life savings, and went out to the Crossroads, the black shanty town on the edge of the city. He purchased books, rugby balls, and cricket bats, and bought land to set up a field with a pitch and touchlines and corner flags. For four years every morning he would make his way out to the Crossroads. He taught children English and how to play rugby and cricket, depending on the season. He befriended the teenagers roaming the streets trying to convince them to get off drugs and avoid crime. When he died in 1994 the funeral of the "Crossroads convert" was attended by over two thousand mourners. Journalists were unable to agree whether there had been more blacks or more whites in the congregation.

A new physical heart from a black man enabled Stoffel to survive four more years. But the new righteous man he became gave him fullness of life for those four years, and forever. A change of heart makes all the difference.

# Hunger and Thirst for Holiness

In St Paul's letters he speaks of the "righteousness of God" which is a gift brought to us by faith. We cannot acquire this righteousness by ourselves but as sheer grace from God which comes through faith in what Jesus has won for us on the Cross (Rom 3:22-26). This frees us from sin and makes us right with God. As important as this teaching from Paul is for our self-understanding it would be wrong to interpret being hungry and thirsty for righteousness as simply seeking God's saving power from sin for ourselves. Having received this saving power through faith it needs to be expressed in works. As James tells us, "faith without works is dead" (James 2:16). The focus of this beatitude is on the deep desire to see things right within all our relationships and in the world at large. It is more about what God requires in our response to his love, than about what God does for us in saving us. It is definitely about our quest for holiness, our yearning for virtue. And this can only come about by the gift of God. But it would be an inadequate response to the challenge of this beatitude to simply seek God's gift of saving grace without thirsting for ways to right the wrongs in the world in which we find ourselves.

This moral righteousness must flow from deeper conversion to God. Jesus says not to worry about what we are to eat and where we are to live and how we are to be clothed. Our heavenly Father knows our needs. We are not to focus so much on *our* needs, but on the needs of *others*. "Seek first his kingdom and his *righteousness* and all these things will be given to you" (Mt 6:33). We must hunger and thirst for a right ordering of relationships according to the way of practical love, mercy and justice. Inner righteousness must cry out on behalf of others who are being abused or misused. When someone in our family, or neighbourhood, or church community is treated unjustly are we ready to speak up on their behalf, even if it will cost us in some way. Are we concerned for the suffering of others? Am I concerned for the spiritual, psychological and material welfare of my neighbour, who doesn't even know me? Some of the issues that may provoke in us a thirst for righteousness would be the protection of human life from conception until death, the plight of refugees throughout the world, the suffering of women and children used in trafficking, the prevalence of abortion, euthanasia, capital punishment. Are we willing to suffer personal inconvenience to stand against and seek to correct any blatant injustice?

Implicit in Jesus' call to "hunger and thirst" for goodness, holiness and righteousness are two assumptions. Firstly, that the desire is as urgent as the hunger pains of someone who is close to physically starving, and the thirst is like someone who is seriously dehydrated, pining for water. We can glean this understanding from the context in which Jesus is speaking where ordinary folk often endured these extreme conditions, which modern Western society has largely alleviated. This gives a greater intensity to the longing and yearning that comes with the grace of this beatitude. Secondly, the blessedness is not about having achieved righteousness, but about thirsting for it. Often we find ourselves before impossible situations where it will take years to right the wrong, and we certainly know in our own personal lives how far we are yet from attaining this level of goodness. Knowing that the blessing is there in the urgent and passionate desire to see things right, even if we fail to ever effect change, is a consolation in itself.

## A Holy Discontent

This beatitude continues in a more active key the previous beatitude about mourning over the trouble in the world. It is about those who can see that our efforts for a more just and equitable world are still not enough; those who are alert and have eyes to see what is lacking, and are in search for something greater; true justice, a right ordering of personal relationships and of relationships in the society at large. They are the sort of people who feel deeply the plight of young men captive to their own passions; suffering from the loss of a father's love, given over to violence and crime due to the wounds of the past. They are the sort of people who are spurred into action when in some parts of the world the rights of women are trampled upon and they are treated as slaves. They are the sort of people who hear the cry of the poor and are not prepared to passively accept the gross inequality built into the world economic system. They are the sort of people who feel the plight of the homeless, the addicted, the refugees, the elderly, the handicapped, and anyone suffering, and are prepared to act on this. They are the sort of people who are not content with the status quo, and are ready to speak challenging words; not afraid to rock the boat when it is necessary, and not afraid to get their hands dirty in humble service of others.

## You Did it to Me

Jesus pronounced basic criteria of judgment which will separate the righteous and the unrighteous at the end of time (Matthew 25: 31-46). The righteous ones (sometimes translated "the virtuous") will be rewarded because they have loved. They will ask, "Lord, when did we see you hungry and feed you; or thirsty and give you drink? When did we see you a stranger and make you welcome; naked and clothe you; sick or in prison and go to see you?" and the King will answer "I tell you solemnly, in so far as you did this to one of these least of my brethren you did it to me". The words of Mother Teresa have power because of her life witness:

> At the end of life we will not be judged by
>> How many diplomas we have received
>> How much money we have made
>> How many great things we have done
>
> We will be judged by
>> "I was hungry and you gave me to eat
>> I was naked and you clothed me
>> I was homeless and you took me in"
>> Hungry not only for bread - but hungry for love
>> Naked not only for clothing – but naked of human dignity and respect
>> Homeless not only for want of a room of bricks – but homeless because of rejection
>
>> This is Christ in the distressing disguise of the poor.

Jesus identified himself with the hungry, the thirsty, the naked, the homeless, the sick and those in prison. Consequently, these are our people. They belong to the Church in a special way, even if they do not profess the faith. In being with the poor we find Jesus in a privileged manner, and if we do not find him in the poor we have not found the kingdom. Pope Francis warns us, "Sometimes we are tempted to be that kind of Christian who keeps the Lord's wounds at arms length. Yet Jesus wants us to touch human misery, to touch the suffering flesh of others."[19] And he assures us that when we come into contact with the sorrowful plight of others we "touch the suffering flesh of Christ". I will return to this perspective when expounding the next beatitude, "Blessed are the merciful". Mother Teresa's focus was passionately for each individual person in need. This was her charism. Ultimately this is what matters most. She was inspired by the cry of Jesus on the Cross, "I thirst!" His thirst for us awakens our thirst for him. But she found this thirst of Christ most compelling in the "distressing disguise of the poor"; she dedicated her life and her congregation to satiating this thirst for love, acceptance, and dignity of the poorest of the poor.

# Pier Giorgio Frassati[20]

During the ceremony in 1990 when Pier Giorgio Frassati was acclaimed as "blessed", Pope John Paul II gave him the title "man of the beatitudes". The particular beatitude that shone most brightly was his hunger and thirst for righteousness. When he died suddenly at the age of 24 years, his wealthy and influential family were not at all prepared for the emotional scenes at his funeral. Thousands of Turin's poor gathered to honour their champion. Pier Giorgio had kept most of his activity with the poor a secret. The family had no idea of the extent of his compassionate work. Pier Giorgio was a fun loving natural prankster amongst his many friends, and had a passion for mountain climbing, geology and photography. But from the age of seventeen he had been secretly visiting the homes of Turin's poor with the Vincent de Paul society. The city teemed with jobless World War I veterans and destitute working families. Pier Giorgio moved daily among them distributing packages of food and clothing, as well as money, usually from his own pocket.

Helping the homeless to find rooms, bringing groceries to hungry families or medicine to those with health issues, he did whatever was necessary to lighten their burden. Usually his visits were before his classes at University or late at night when he could get away from his duties. Whenever gifts or money came his way from his wealthy father he would bring them to the poor. The living conditions of the people he served were in stark contrast to his own lodgings at his parent's house. When a friend asked why he did not find the filth repugnant he replied, "Jesus comes to me every morning in Holy Communion. I repay him in my very small way by visiting the poor. The house may be sordid, but I am going to Christ." The joy which sustained him flowed from his intimacy with Christ. He nourished this intimacy with daily Mass and overnight vigils of adoration before the Blessed Sacrament. "After a prayer vigil" he said, "I feel stronger, safer, more secure, and even happier."

Pier Giorgio also had a heart for justice. As a young university student he could see that social and economic change were needed to relieve the causes of poverty. He decided to major in mechanical engineering with the hope of working with miners, who in those days were particularly disadvantaged. When Mussolini's Fascist party rose to power in Italy, Pier Giorgio more than once risked his life by publicly opposing the regime. He was bashed a few times during anti-fascist demonstrations. His love for the poor guided his political choices. He fought to build a better society that would bring justice to the oppressed. He was bitterly disappointed when some Church officials supported Mussolini. He said, "It is better to stand alone with a clean conscience than to stand with all the rest, but with a stain on our conscience."

Pier Giorgio enjoyed life to the full, and his greatest joy of all was to give to others, to the point of heroic sacrifice. The polio which killed him was contracted during his many visits to the poor. Even on his death bed he was giving instructions about medicine for a sick man and the need to renew an insurance policy for another on his behalf. Pier Giorgio's great heart made him hunger and thirst for righteousness, and now the Church has recognised his holiness. The most striking feature of his character is his joyful love for Christ, whom he found in music, art and poetry, and in the high mountains, but most of all in the poor.

## A Thirst for Justice

We have seen that those who hunger and thirst for righteousness cannot passively stand apart when they encounter injustice. They have God's heart for the oppressed and will throw themselves into making things right, no matter what the cost. When Oscar Romero was made Archbishop of San Salvador in February 1977 his appointment was welcomed by the government and the rich oligarchies. He was seen to be conservative and someone who would not challenge the status quo. His appointment was met with dismay by those radical priests who had aligned themselves with violent ideologies in frustration at the Church's silence and passivity in the face of grave social injustices. However, while Romero was still bishop of Santiago de Maria, before his elevation to being Archbishop, he had already begun to question the situation. He was horrified that children were dying because parents could not afford simple medicines. The landless poor did not have the means for basic survival, while the rich who controlled the land were living in luxury.

A month after being appointed Archbishop a good friend of his, Fr Rutilio Grande, who was working closely with the poor was assassinated, together with two of his parishioners. Fr Rutilio was not a Marxist but was a humble Jesuit priest helping his people in the poor *campesinos* to become more self-reliant and develop a sustainable livelihood. Standing at the place where the atrocity occurred Romero was faced with a decision which would shape the rest of his life. This untimely death of his friend was a divine catalyst. He knew now he had to make a decisive option for the poor. Later he said, "When I looked at Rutilio lying there dead I thought 'if they have killed him for doing what he did, then I too have to walk the same path'". A deeply spiritual man, he cried out to the Lord to seek his will. He felt confirmation from God that, helpless though he was before the powerful forces of an oppressive government which supported the elite rich, he must become the "voice of the voiceless" and speak against the injustice. Later he was to say, "There are many things that can only be seen through eyes that have cried." The following Sunday he cancelled all Masses in the Archdiocese and invited all to come the Cathedral Square where he celebrated one single Mass before 100,000 people. He refused to participate in any official government ceremonies until the assassins were brought to justice. He did not incite the violence of hatred, but what he called "the violence of love", which means dying to self with Jesus on the Cross for the sake of others. As he proclaimed:

> We have never preached violence, except the violence of love, which left Christ nailed to a cross, the violence that we must each do to ourselves to overcome our selfishness and such cruel inequalities among us. The violence we preach is not the violence of the sword, the violence of hatred. It is the violence of love, of brotherhood, the violence that wills to beat weapons into sickles for work.[21]

As the killings increased, he opened a diocesan office to document the murders, disappearances and tortures, and to offer support for the families of victims. His weekly sermons were broadcast by radio throughout the country. He preached the gospel uncompromisingly, and wrote pastoral letters of solidarity. He spoke against the enforced poverty of the people, the gross economic injustice, the assassinations and torture. During his three years as archbishop fifty priests were attacked, threatened or slandered. Six of them died as martyrs, having been assassinated. Religious women were persecuted. The Catholic radio station, Catholic schools and universities and other institutions were constantly attacked, menaced and threatened with bombs. He became the voice of his people. Again and again he denounced the idolatory of wealth and land, the idolatory of power and national "security", and the idolatory of political ideology. He called all to repentance.

Romero spoke from the heart of the suffering Church, enduring the passion of Jesus and sharing in his Cross:

> For the Church, the many abuses of human life, liberty, and dignity are a heartfelt suffering. The Church, entrusted with the earth's glory, believes that in each person is the Creator's image and that everyone who tramples it offends God. As holy defender of God's rights and of his images, the Church must cry out. It takes as spittle on its face, as lashes on its back, as the Cross in its passion, all that human beings suffer, even though they be unbelievers. They suffer as God's image. There is no dichotomy between

man and God's image. Whoever tortures a human being, whoever abuses a human being, whoever outrages a human being abuses God's image, and the Church takes as its own that Cross, that martyrdom.[22]

Romero also spoke as the prophet in his land. Like the prophets of old, on behalf of the Church he "called a spade a spade", and confronted the elite and powerful of the land with their sin, calling them to repent.

> The Church must suffer for speaking the truth, for pointing out sin, for uprooting sin. No one wants to have a sore spot touched, and therefore a society with so many sores twitches when someone has the courage to touch it.....
>
> A church that does not provoke crisis, that preaches a gospel which does not unsettle, that proclaims the word of God which does not get under anyone's skin, or a word of God that does not touch the real sin of the society in which it is proclaimed: what kind of gospel is that?[23]

Inevitably on March 24 1980 an assassin fired a fatal shot from the door of the chapel where Romero was celebrating Mass. He had just finished a homily in which he had said:

> Those who surrender to the service of the poor through love of Christ, will live like the grain of wheat that dies. If it were not to die it would remain a solitary grain. The harvest comes because of the grain that dies. We know that every effort to improve society, above all when society is so full of injustice and sin, is an effort that God blesses; that God wants; that God demands of us.

In the film entitled *Romero*, with a little poetic licence, the bullet went through his chest while he was elevating the chalice after the consecration. As he fell to the floor his own blood was mingled with the blood of Jesus; an apt description of a life fully given to God for the sake of his people, sharing in the sacrifice of Christ for all.

## Blessed are You Hungry

Luke's beatitude is more direct. "Blessed are *you* who hunger now, you shall be satisfied." We immediately think of the millions of people who die of hunger, many of them children, while the rich stuff themselves with more food to the point of obesity. We think of the tons of good food thrown out as waste in most of the cities of the Western world, while Lazarus is at the door desperate for the scraps from our table. Jesus follows this with "Woe to you who have your fill now, you will be hungry". It leads us to re-visit the parable of the rich man and Lazarus, which indicates graphically the plight of those who are rich and indifferent to the hungry of this world. While they have a "good life" now, after death they will be forever crying out for just a drop of water to quench their thirst.

This is a wake-up call for many of us. Satiety has a way of dulling the mind and hardening the heart. Wealth, and the satisfactions it brings, keep us captive to an earthly mentality. We do not want to share what we have. We need to be shocked out of our complacency and hardness of heart. Recently I stood in a refugee camp in Uganda watching young children clambering for any piece of clothing they could claim as their own from the relatively meagre amount we had brought with us. And then to my dismay I watched the children eagerly picking up from the dust some of the maize which had fallen from our now empty sacks. We had brought something but it was not enough. I stood helplessly in tears and knew that by his providence God was allowing me to experience his heart as he weeps for his little ones. The comparison between what these people were daily suffering and the way of life that we take for granted was so stark I was shaken to the core. This sort of experience is life-changing. We cannot be the same again, but must respond.

James addresses the rich, saying "Come now, you rich, weep and howl for the miseries that are coming upon you. Your riches have rotted" (James 5:1-2). The coming of the Kingdom of God has turned everything upside down. Mary's Magnificat expresses it beautifully, "He has filled the hungry with good things, and the rich he has sent empty away." This is the heart of God. He is for the poor. The gospel does not condemn people for being rich, but if they are accumulating wealth for its own sake and ignoring the plight of the hungry and the poor, they are warned that things will not go well for them in the end. The gospel of the poor is a reversal of values that the capitalistic world finds difficult to comprehend. That is why some brands of Christianity promote a prosperity gospel, preferring to draw from Old Testament texts rather than from the preaching of Jesus. It is an illusory message and an abomination of the truth. The gospel reveals a new kind of wealth which is not dependent on material prosperity at all. That is why the poor are called blessed. "God has chosen those who are poor in the world to be rich in faith and heirs of the kingdom" (James 2:5).

There is something wrong globally when one third of the world is consuming 85 per cent of the resources. And there is something askew when one fourth of the food produced by that privileged one third is thrown out as waste. If it was salvaged it would go a long way to solving the problem of world hunger. It is good to let down our defences and get in touch with the dreadful misery in the world, and to feel uneasy in a healthy and constructive way about it. St John Chrysostom says, "Not to enable the poor to share in our goods is to steal from them and deprive them of life. The goods we possess are not ours, but theirs."[24] He is saying that it is not a matter of us kindly offering our surplus from a sentimental motive. Rather it is a matter of justice demanded by God. Gregory the Great says, "When we attend to the needs of those in want, we give them what is theirs, not ours. More than performing works of mercy, we are paying a debt of justice."[25] James is always straight to the point. He says, "If one of the brothers or sisters is in need of clothes and has not enough food to live on, and one of you says to them, 'I wish you well; keep yourself warm and eat plenty', without giving them these bare necessities of life, then what good is that?" (James 2:15-16)

When Archbishop Oscar Romero was asked to explain the phrase "option for the poor" he replied by giving an example. Imagine a building is on fire and you are watching it burn, wondering if everyone is safe. Then someone tells you that your mother and your sister are inside the building. Your attitude changes completely. You're frantic; your mother and sister are burning and you would do anything to rescue them even at the cost of being burnt yourself. That, he said, is what it means to be truly committed:

If we look at poverty from the outside, as if we are just looking at the fire, that's not to opt for the poor, no matter how concerned we may be. We must get inside as if our own mother and sister were burning. Indeed it is Christ who is there, hungry and suffering.

# 5
# BLESSED ARE THE MERCIFUL

*Blessed are the merciful, for they will receive mercy Mt 5:7*

Mercy is the highest quality in the heart of God. His name is mercy.[26] Any true follower of Jesus will have this heart of mercy. It is a gift from God which does not come naturally to fallen humanity. If we are governed by our natural reactions we will be harsh towards others who don't match up to our expectations, and when we have been offended by them we will more than likely be spiteful and vindictive, seeking revenge. This is not the heart of God revealed in Jesus. Only when we experience God's mercy will we grow in compassion for others. This is one of the greatest challenges of adult life. Many refuse to let their hearts be softened and remain outside of God's mercy. In the first letter of Peter, which was most likely a baptismal catechesis, defining who we are as followers of Jesus, the author says: "Once you were not a people, but now you are God's people; once you had not received mercy, but now you have received mercy" (1Pet 2:10). As the community of Christ's disciples our deepest identity is that we are the people who have received mercy. Because of this, we can have the heart of Jesus to freely bestow mercy.

## The Merciful Gaze of Jesus

Pope Francis has often related his early encounter with the mercy of God which changed his life forever. At the age of 17 years, on the feast of St Matthew, he went to the sacrament of Reconciliation. After confessing his sins and receiving absolution he felt deeply the touch of God's mercy, which was unearned and undeserved, a sheer gift with no strings attached. That is why as bishop and then as Pope he chose the motto: *"miserando atque eligendo"*. It is taken from the reflections of Bede the Venerable on the calling of Matthew. Roughly translated from the Latin it means: "gazing upon him with mercy he called him". The young Jorge Bergoglio experienced what Matthew felt when he was called by Jesus. Matthew was one of the tax collectors, who were despised by the Jewish people. They collected heavy taxes from the Roman occupying power and were free to add their own commission for their own gain. They were shunned by others and spent their ill-gotten money on parties and prostitutes. But there was something in the gaze of Jesus that opened Matthew's heart; it was tender mercy. Unworthy as he was, Jesus called him to be a disciple. This is how Pope Francis feels. Early in his pontificate when he was asked by a journalist, "Who is Jorge Bergoglio?" Without a moment's hesitation he answered, "He is a sinner who has met the mercy of Christ". That is why, after receiving the sacrament of mercy at the tender age of 17, he responded to the call to become a Jesuit.

## One with Sinners

The Pharisees in the gospels could not understand this. After Matthew responded to the call of the Lord he invited Jesus to a party put on by his disreputable friends and associates. The Pharisees were scandalised that Jesus would welcome tax-collectors and public sinners and share table fellowship with them. Jesus replied, "It is not the healthy who need the doctor, but the sick. Go and learn the meaning of the words: What I want is mercy, not sacrifice. And indeed I did not come to call the virtuous, but sinners" (Mt 9:10-13). Maybe in each of our hearts there lurks something of this Pharisaical attitude, which hardens us against mercy. We may not be blatantly proud, arrogant and self-righteous. But in a more subtle way we can feel superior to those who have lost their way in a confused mire of sinful pursuits. We can take the higher moral ground and look down our noses in judgement and condemnation upon those who have failed miserably in keeping God's law.

If we do not recognise our need for "the doctor" then Jesus can have no part with us. If we cannot admit our own sinfulness, then we have no need of the Saviour. If we think we have it all together and can make judgements on others then we are the self-made virtuous ones who shut themselves out of the Father's house. Consequently, like the Pharisees, we will not have mercy in our hearts for others.

Jesus told a parable for those who trust in their own virtue, and have a hidden sense of superiority in their heart towards others (Lk 18: 9-14). Two men went up to the Temple to pray. The first, a Pharisee, stood at the front before God and prayed, "God I thank you that I am not like other people: thieves, rogues, adulterers, or even like this tax-collector." Then he listed his "sacrifices" – fasting twice a week, tithing. The tax-collector, down the back, not even able to lift his eyes towards heaven, but just beating his breast, cried, "God be merciful to me a sinner!" That prayer pleased the Lord. The other did not. Why? The tax-collector's prayer was real. It was honest. He didn't have any spiritual achievements or claims to virtue. Yet he was standing in truth, without any pretence. There was no cover-up, no social or religious mask; simply the raw reality of his weak, wounded and shabby condition before God. All he could do was trust in God's mercy.

## The Joy in the Father's House

The well known parable of the prodigal son was told by Jesus to address the Pharisees. They complained that if Jesus was a holy man, how could he welcome sinners and eat with them?

The story draws a contrast between the merciful attitude of the Father, and the hard heart of the older brother, who refused to forgive. The younger son had offended the father deeply. By asking for his inheritance he was saying, "I wish you were dead". The Father, did not refuse him, but gave him his freedom. The young man cut loose from his family home and land. He plunged into the world and squandered everything on the proverbial "wine, women and song". Ending up penniless and in shame, working in a pig sty, and longing to eat their scraps, he comes to his senses, and makes his way home to the Father's house. He expected at best to be treated as a hired servant. But all this time the Father has been waiting for him, longing for his return. When he sees him in the distance he forgets his dignity, hitches up his long robes, and runs to his son. He does not worry about the smell of the pigs, but throws his arms around his son and kisses him tenderly. This is the merciful heart of God. He did not ask questions: how many women? What happened to the money? He is full of joy at the sons return. He does not count his faults against him. He orders a celebration. God's mercy is totally gratuitous.

In contrast to the Father's mercy, the older son cannot join the celebration. He condemns his brother for his faults. He represents the Pharisees who complained about Jesus eating with sinners. He has been the dutiful one, law-abiding and respected, admired and praised for his virtue, but he lacks the quality of mercy. In his self-righteousness and resentful anger he shuts himself out from the Father's house and refuses to share in the joy. The Father comes out to plead with him to come in to the celebration of mercy. The older son bitterly recounts to the Father how he has been so hard-working, and of upstanding character, and feels unappreciated. His recrimination towards his brother has given rise to self-pity. He refers to his brother as "this son of yours" who has wasted the Father's money on loose women. We must notice that the Father loves this older son as much as the one who has returned. He says, "My son", which in the original language is more like "my dear child", "you are with me always and all I have is yours". The Father's heart is full of generosity. He pleads with his son not to shut himself out from the joy. His brother "was dead and has come back to life; he was lost and is found".

The plight of the older son is that of good religious people who are so intent upon their performance in the house of God that they have become proud and self-sufficient. They have lost touch with their own weakness and nothingness before God, and hence they do not know how much they need his mercy. Consequently, they hold back from bringing mercy to others. Instead they demand justice alone.

# Why Forgive?

If we are growing in a merciful heart we will have the grace to forgive those who have offended us. We naturally resist forgiving someone who has wounded us. We don't want to let people off the hook so easily. People will espouse many reasons why they cannot or will not forgive. "I don't want to encourage irresponsibility", "I want him to suffer for a while, since he caused me to suffer", "I am the victim; she needs to face the consequences of her actions", "He is not sorry so how can I possibly forgive?" "It just is not fair to have to forgive". Yet when Jesus was asked by Peter "How many time should we forgive, seven times?" Jesus answered emphatically, "Not seven times, but seventy seven times", which was a Semitic way of saying always without exceptions. Then he proceeded to explain why we must forgive, and indeed how we can do such an unthinkable thing.

He told the parable of a servant who owed his master, the king, ten thousand talents, which is the equivalent in today's currency of about six million dollars. The king demanded payment, otherwise he and his family would be thrown into prison. The man fell at his master's feet and pleaded to give him time to be able to pay back the debt. The king was so moved by his request that he cancelled the debt. What a relief that must have been to the man, and surely he would have immense gratitude for such a gift. But we are told the man went out and accosted a fellow servant who owed him a hundred denarii, the equivalent of a measly ten dollars. He began to throttle the man and threatened to throw him and his family into prison until he had paid back the debt. When the king heard about his he was angry at the ungrateful servant. He had him thrown out to the torturers.

I will come back to explain the part about the torturers. First let's gain the central point of the parable. The king, through his mercy, as sheer gift, cancelled the debt of the servant which was utterly impossible for him to pay. This is what Jesus has done for us when he hung on the Cross for our sake. The debt owing to our sin was completely beyond our means to pay; infinitely more than six million dollars. It is conceivable that the man in the parable may have been able to raise six million dollars somehow; but it is totally inconceivable that we could have earned our salvation. It is sheer gift from God. Paul tells us God was "rich in mercy... because it is by grace that you have been saved, through faith; not by anything of your own, but by a gift from God" (Eph 2: 4,8). We have an immense debt of gratitude to God for his mercy. This should motivate us to have mercy on others. The servant in the story had received so much, but he would give nothing. That's why he lost his master's favour. The offences made against us by others, even though they may cut deeply, are nothing in comparison with the offences made against God by the human race. But in his mercy by hanging on the Cross for us he has "cancelled every record of the debt that we had to pay" (Col 2: 14). We have received freely, and consequently, we should give freely (cf. Mt 10:8).

## The Torture of Resentment

It is significant in the parable that the unforgiving man should be thrown to the torturers. The most tortured people I have met are those who will not forgive. They carry a cancer of resentment within them that is slowly killing them. It is a poison in the soul, which can distort one's whole interior life. It is a sickness that begins in the spirit, but then influences the mind and emotions, and can even manifest in the body. It is a major source of psychosomatic illnesses. Physical disorders such as stomach ulcers, high blood pressure, depression, nightmares, excessive stress, arthritis and many other conditions can originate in buried resentment. More than once when praying for healing we have been presented with a serious physical or emotional condition only to be led by the Holy Spirit to the root cause of the problem being a refusal to forgive someone. If the person who is suffering forgives then the healing can happen.

## The Choice to Forgive

When we forgive we choose to let go of the clenched fist which we are holding up inside ourselves against another. It is a willingness to let go of the past hurts and not keep nursing them endlessly. It is a choice to withdraw the judgments we have made on others and to leave their judgment to God. It is a choice to extend mercy and to be generous to those who do not deserve it. It is a choice to stop blaming others for the unfortunate and painful episodes of our life. Even if our feelings towards the one who offended us are negative, and we have anger within us towards them, we can still move under grace and choose to forgive. The feelings can catch up later. If the offence has been great, such as a breach of trust, then we may find we have to keep making the decision each day until the heart catches up. I would encourage a daily prayer asking the Lord for the grace of forgiveness, using your will to make the choice, and then before God stating the forgiveness explicitly.

## A Life Restored by Forgiveness

Elaine's life turned into a nightmare on 17 August 2000. Her sister, Adelia, and partner, died when their house burnt to the ground. The fire had been deliberately lit as a vengeful murder. Thankfully the three children were saved, and now Elaine was caring for them. The cruel loss of her sister, who was a "soul-mate", weighed heavily on Elaine. She hated the murderer with a passion, and when he was arrested, and sentenced to life in prison, she wished the worst for him. Tormented within her soul she arrived at a healing Mass and the celebrant was preaching on forgiveness. After the Mass she accosted the priest angrily, thinking that he must have had prior knowledge of her situation, since the homily had spoken directly to her heart. Her face was contorted and, wringing her hands angrily, she told the priest she never could forgive the man who murdered her sister. The priest gently encouraged her that unless she forgave him, the deep wound inside her would fester and never be healed. The wound, he explained, was like a cancer that starts small but gets bigger until all her energy would be wasted on hating this man. She listened but stomped off determined never to forgive.

In the meantime, Elaine seemed to be hearing from all sides the voice of the Lord through others. Her husband reckoned the priest had a good point. There was a story in the newspaper about someone who forgave a murderer. Her counsellor suggested "I think someone is trying to tell you something.

Are you listening?" So she turned up to another healing Mass. This time, without knowing she was present, the priest led the congregation through a forgiveness prayer. As she listened, it did not seem to apply to her. But then towards the end the priest had people pray: "Heavenly Father, I especially pray for the grace of forgiveness for that one person in life who has hurt me the most. I ask to be able to forgive anyone whom I consider my greatest enemy, the one who is the hardest to forgive or the one whom I said I would never forgive. Thank you, Father, that I am free of the evil of unforgiveness. Let your Holy Spirit fill me with light and let every dark area of my mind be enlightened. In Jesus' name. Amen".

Elaine felt immediately she had to go to the sacrament of Reconciliation to ask the Lord's forgiveness for her hatred, and to gain the power to forgive her sister's murderer. The priest led her through a forgiveness prayer. She recalls, "I felt a great weight lifted from me". Elaine realized that she had become a victim through her refusal to forgive, and her hate had separated her from God. Forgiveness set her free. She had been bound up inside herself by her enmity towards the murderer. Now, through forgiveness a new light came into her eyes, and a shining smile on her face, and a whole new freshness in her demeanour. When we forgive we share in the peace of Christ.

## Breaking the Cycle of Violence

In the face of the worst possible injustice towards us, the only way to freedom is by forgiveness. Without forgiveness our lives are governed by hatred and revenge. We are captive to the dark forces unleashed by the original violence. We buy into the law of revenge and we end up oppressors ourselves. As Mahatma Ghandi once declared: "If we all live by 'eye for an eye' the whole world will be blind". The only way through is forgiveness. Otherwise we contribute to the cycle of violence. If a person hurts me and I retaliate, I think it only fair to hit back harder. Then that person will feel justified to strike back even harder again. There is an ever-increasing cycle of violence that threatens to escalate perpetually. Forgiveness breaks the cycle of violence. It frees us from the endless chain of reactions. Even if we are disciplined enough to limit our retaliation to an equitable level by simply giving "tit" for "tat", which was the original meaning of "eye for an eye", does that really help in the long run? Do we really feel better if we rage at another driver and deliberately cut in front of him with abusive hand signals? Are we really better off when we pay back someone by pouring verbal abuse upon them? Our grievance and revenge hurts others, and this new hurt further feeds their anger and vengeance, fuelling endless pain.

## The Cross of Jesus brings Freedom

The power of the Cross of Jesus is our liberation. It speaks of the rich mercy of God. God is not indifferent to our conflicts. He became one of us and entered into our mess to set us free. When Jesus was being nailed to the Cross he did not rise up and smite the soldiers who were unjustly inflicting excruciating pain upon him. Instead, at that very moment he cried out, "Father, forgive them, for they know not what they do". These words, from his heart broken open in love for us, have breathed life into our world, giving us new hope that we are not doomed to an endless cycle of violence. On the Cross goodness conquered evil, and love conquered hatred. Now, if we are prepared to draw strength from the Cross of Jesus, the creative power of forgiveness is always available, even when grave injustice has been done to us. On the Cross Jesus turned what was the worst form of human condemnation, torture and execution, into a permanent sign of the enduring merciful love of God.

When we are finding it difficult to forgive, it can be helpful to imagine ourselves at the foot of the Cross of Jesus together with the person we need to forgive. Standing with the offender, looking up at the crucified Jesus, who is enduring this agony for each one of us, we realize that it is only by the mercy of God that any of us can stand at all. As the psalmist says, "If you O Lord should mark our guilt who would survive? But with you is found forgiveness, for this we revere you" (Ps 130:3-4). Standing at the foot of the Cross we become aware that it is only by the blood of Jesus shed for each of us that we have been saved. Otherwise our lives would be hopelessly shipwrecked. We can allow the precious blood of Jesus to soften our hearts and empower us to forgive and let go the judgements and resentment.

## A Heart of Mercy

Margaret Mizen, a mother of nine from South London, suffered grievously when she rushed to the local bakery after hearing that her sixteen-year-old son Jimmy had been attacked. When she arrived she found him dead in his brother's arms. He had been killed by a shard of glass bashed over his head, which had cut his throat and caused him to bleed to death almost instantly. The assailant was another teenager who had tried to pick a fight with Jimmy's brother. When Jimmy had tried to cool them down, the angry youth launched his deadly attack. Margaret and her husband Barry are devoted Catholics. Jimmy was still an altar boy.

Later when the TV cameras arrived, Margaret and Barry granted an interview. Margaret said her heart was broken, but she was most concerned for the mother of the boy who had murdered her son. She said she and her husband had wonderful memories of their son. "He was a dear, dear sweet young man, we loved him dearly". But she felt sorry for the mother of the murderer. With a merciful heart she said, "What can we really say to them? They must be in so much pain. We want them to know that we forgive." People could not understand why they would not be angry and seek revenge. She made it clear that if she "gave in" to that temptation she would just add to the violence and be doing exactly what her son's murderer had done. She refused to be caught up in the cycle of violence. What a beautiful Christian witness! We proclaim that without mercy we are lost, without forgiveness we have no future.

## Works of Mercy

"Blessed are the merciful" also refers to those who engage in corporal works of mercy. God is crying out to each one of us, as he did to Cain, "Where is your brother?" (Gen 4:9). Cain's reply was "I do not know, am I my brother's keeper?" The answer to this question is "yes, you are". And so for each one of us. A story is told of Pope John XXIII when he was Archbishop Angelo Roncalli. One of the priests under his care had fallen into trouble and the Archbishop's advisers were wanting him to take drastic punitive measures. The future Pope lifted up a wine goblet and asked them, "Whose is this wine glass?" They replied, "Yours, your Excellency." Then he threw it down on the stone floor and it shattered into pieces. "Whose is it now?" he asked. Startled, they replied, "Yours, your Excellency." Then he continued, "And that is how it is with my brother. Whether he is all together, or whether he is broken and shattered, he is still my brother." And so it is with all our brothers and sisters in the human race. The world is desperately in need of this attitude of mercy. This is the true face of the Church, which people need to discover.

When a lawyer asked Jesus what must I do to inherit eternal life, Jesus asked him "what do you find in the Law?" The man answered "You must love the Lord your God with all your heart and all your soul, with all your strength, and with all your mind, and your neighbour as yourself". Jesus affirmed him saying "You have answered right, do this and life is yours". But the lawyer pushed with a further question, which provoked a surprising answer, "And who is my neighbour?" Jesus answered with the parable of the good Samaritan. We know it well, and it continues to challenge us. A man going down on foot from Jerusalem to Jericho was attacked by robbers. They took all he had, beat him, and left him half dead. A priest came by but passed him on the other side of the road, pretending not to see him. A Levite, another well respected religious man, came by and likewise avoided getting involved. Then a Samaritan, one of the "half-caste" breed despised by the Jews, came by, and was moved with compassion for him. The Greek word here suggests that he was stirred at gut level with mercy, such that he could not be indifferent to this man's plight. He went up to the man, bandaged his wounds, lifted him onto his mount, took him to an inn and looked after him. Jesus asked the lawyer, "which one proved to be the man's neighbour?" "The one who had mercy on him" he replied. Jesus said to him, "Go and do the same yourself".

## In the Slums of Calcutta

We have many shining examples of this heart of mercy. On 10th September 1946 Mother Teresa, a Loreto sister was travelling by train to her annual retreat. She received what she referred to later as "a call within a call". She said "when that happens the only thing to do is to say 'yes'". She knew without doubt she was to give up everything to follow Jesus into the slums of Calcutta, and to serve him in the poorest of the poor.[27] It took a couple of years to gain permission, but with great courage and trust in the Lord she began. One day while on the streets of Calcutta she saw a dying woman who had been half eaten by rats and ants. She picked her up, brought her to a hospital, but the hospital could not do anything for the dying woman. Undaunted, Mother Teresa went straight to the city hall and asked the authorities to give her a place where she could bring these dying people who filled the streets. The city health officer took Mother to an abandoned Kali temple. In earlier times Hindus would worship Kali, the goddess of death, in this place as they were preparing their dead. She gladly accepted the offer of the building. Within 24 hours she had dying people there. Mother Teresa said, "The most prevalent disease today is not leprosy or tuberculosis, but rather the feeling of being unwanted, uncared for, deserted by everybody." She felt called by the Lord to "satiate the thirst of Jesus" by loving Jesus in the "distressing disguise of the poor". That was the beginning of her Home for the Dying.

Mother Teresa told this story: "I once picked up a woman from the garbage dump and she was burning with fever. She was in her last days and her only lament was: 'My son did this to me'. I begged her, 'You must forgive your son. In a moment of madness when he was not himself he did a thing he regrets. Be a mother to him. Forgive him'. It took me a long time to make her say, 'I forgive my son'. Just before she died in my arms she was able to say that with real forgiveness. She was not concerned that she was dying. The breaking of her heart was that her son did not want her. This is something you and I can understand." In caring for the destitute and dying she was not able to keep them alive, but she was able to help them die with dignity knowing they were loved.

Mother Teresa often related another story about a man whom the Sisters had picked up from the drain, half eaten with worms, and had brought to the Home for the Dying. The man was not bitter, but happy and grateful knowing that he was going to die at least with someone loving him. She said, "It was so good to see the greatness of that man who could speak like that, who could die like that without blaming anybody without cursing anybody, without comparing anything. Like an angel – this is the greatness of the people". For Mother Teresa the poor offer us so much that can heal our hearts if we are open to it. Most of all when we look into the eyes of a suffering one we are looking into the eyes of Christ; as we touch and seek to bring comfort we are touching the broken, bruised body of Christ. This she reminds us is a beautiful privilege.

## Healed by the Touch of Mercy

Francis of Assisi was a high-spirited young man and often the life of the party. But his heart was changing. Experience of suffering as a prisoner of war opened him more to God. And a dream he received at Spoleto, after he had gallantly set out to fight for the papal armies, led him to return home to Assisi to wait on the Lord. God was preparing him for the encounter that would change his life. One day Francis was riding by himself in the area around Assisi. There in front of him stood a man in rags and with the swollen face of a leper. Francis was horrified. He drew his reins to turn the horse around and ride away as quickly as he could. Lepers frightened him to death. Then came the moment of grace. He stopped the horse. Got down and, shuddering within himself at the sweet decision he had made, he advanced towards the leper. He took the hand of the leper and pressed it to his lips. With fear and passion he kissed the leper. A few days later he came to the leper colony with a large sum of money and kissed the hands of each one. He recalled in his *Testament* that "When I had become acquainted with them, what had previously nauseated me became a source of spiritual and physical consolation for me."[28]

Later when he had brothers they used to take care of leprosy patients and sick people in the hospital. There was one man suffering from leprosy who was so irritable and impatient that no one wanted to care for him.[29] They thought that because of his horrible foul language and barrages of insults that he was possessed by an evil spirit. He would blaspheme and curse the holy name of Jesus, and that of Our Lady and the saints. He had been abandoned by the friars since they couldn't endure his behaviour. After discovering the problem Francis went to the man and greeted him, "God give you peace, my dear brother". The man answered reproachfully: "What peace can I have from God. He has taken from me all peace and everything that is good, and has made me all rotten and stinking?"

Francis could sense the presence of an evil spirit, so he went aside for a while to intercede in prayer. He came back and offered to care for the man. He told him he would do whatever he wanted. The man wailed that the Friars had given up on him and said, "I want you to wash me all over, because I smell so bad that I can't stand it myself." Francis then gently undressed the man and began to wash him tenderly with scented warm water. Wherever Francis touched the man he was healed. As the man began to see the healing taking place in his body he began to weep for his sins and repent for his foul behaviour. He was cleansed not only of leprosy on the outside but also the leprosy of the soul that was even more deadly. The mercy of God in the heart of Francis flowed over as he lovingly cleansed the wounds of this wretched man, changing his heart forever.

## Weeping with Compassion

This beatitude links closely with "blessed are they who mourn". The merciful know how to weep, and they see things as they face reality through tears of compassion. Often in the gospels Jesus is moved deeply by the plight of others. He is not indifferent. Pope Francis shook the complacency of the world, when early in his pontificate he visited Lampedusa, a naturally beautiful Italian island in the Mediterranean Sea, which had been overwhelmed by the tragedy of countless untimely deaths. The Pope came to mourn over the dead bodies of many refugees from north Africa who had drowned when their flimsy boats had sunk before they reached the island, leaving them no chance of survival. In an impassioned plea to the world, which had been watching this disaster unfold, the Pope asked in his homily, "Has any one of us grieved for the death of these brothers and sisters? Has any one of us wept for these persons who were on the boat? For the young mothers carrying their babies? For these men who were looking for a means of support for their families?" He was challenging the culture of comfort which breeds an attitude of indifference to the suffering of the poor; a culture whereby we live in an insulated bubble, insensitive to the cries of those in dire need. We shirk from accepting responsibility for the suffering of others; we say "it does not affect me; it doesn't concern me; it's none of my business!" He laments, "We are a society which has forgotten how to weep, how to experience compassion, which means 'suffering with' others: the globalization of indifference has taken from us the ability to weep!"

## The Merciful Heart of Jesus

The heart of Jesus is otherwise. In the Hebrew mentality the most intense human feelings are not associated with the physical heart, but located in the pit of the stomach. Jesus was moved with compassion in a 'gut wrenching' way many times. We will reflect upon just two of these moments. A leper came up to Jesus and pleaded on his knees: "If you want to you can cure me". In that society lepers were pariahs, having to keep at a safe distance and shouting out "Unclean!" "Unclean!", in order to warn people to stay clear. They dwelt together in colonies isolated from the rest of the society. But Jesus, undaunted, deeply moved in his stomach with compassion for this wretched man, stretched out his hand and touched him. That was a taboo gesture. Never touch a leper! It was a touch of mercy, of solidarity with this man in his affliction, unconcerned for the possibility of incurring the disease himself. The mercy of Jesus was such that he so identified with the most outcast and marginalised in the society he became one of them. On the Cross, Jesus became the ultimate "leper", taking upon himself the "leprosy" of our sin that we may be healed. So in this sweet gospel encounter Jesus says, "Of course I want to! Be healed!" The leprosy left the man immediately. This is the heart that, as we have seen, Francis of Assisi showed to the lepers in his day.

At another time Jesus had escaped in the boat to a lonely place with his disciples to have some rest from the excessive apostolic pressures. To his great surprise, and to the dismay of his disciples, people had guessed where they were heading, and using another route arrived there before them. When he looked out upon the crowd gathered before them, Jesus was moved in the pit of the stomach again. He could not leave the people without a word of hope (Mk 6:30-34). Then after a long day of teaching he was moved to feed them. When the apostles protested there was nowhere to buy food, he said, "give them something to eat yourselves". He wanted the disciples to share his heart, and to do as he would do. They knew it was impossible to feed these people. It would cost too much to buy the food, and in any case it was deserted place. Jesus asked them to bring what they had. Five loaves and two fish was the total amount available. What was that amongst so many? Jesus had the crowd sit down, and then, raising his eyes to heaven, and praying a thanksgiving prayer, he broke the loaves and handed them to the disciples to distribute. The miracle happened at the hands of the disciples; more and more bread kept coming. Jesus was teaching them that a heart of mercy is not paralysed by feelings of apathy, indifference, and a sense of helplessness, but confidently acts with what is readily available, and God will make up the difference.

# 6
# BLESSED ARE THE PURE OF HEART

*Blessed are the pure of heart, for they will see God  Mt 5: 8*

## Single-minded for God

The pure of heart are those who are single-mindedly for God. In the New Testament the Greek word "*katharos*", for pure, refers not only to the virtue of chastity but to a quality which should permeate all the other virtues as well. The pure of heart want union with God and they are willing to forsake everything else for this one ultimate goal. Psalm 24 is a good starting point to consider this beatitude: "Who shall climb the mountain of the Lord? Who shall stand in his holy place? The man with clean hands and pure heart, who desires not worthless things…Such are the men who seek him, seek the face of the God of Jacob" (Ps 24: 3-4,6). It is a matter of the desires of the heart, of which there are many. What do I desire most in life? What drives me forward? What motivates me?

St Augustine speaks to the issue: "You have created us for yourself, O Lord, and our hearts are restless until they rest in you." For Augustine the whole Christian life is one uninterrupted desire for God. He teaches that the entire journey is simply a holy yearning for union with the Lord. We are to pray always since this is the underlying current of our lives, a heartfelt longing for God. Our times of prayer simply bring to the surface that basic orientation of the deep hunger for God which is written into our nature. Those who are pure of heart passionately love God with all their heart, soul, mind and strength. This God-directed desire for union with him is a quiet, but consistent fire within the soul; what Jeremiah called "a fire imprisoned in my bones" which could not be constrained, even when he was enduring hardship and persecution (Jer 20:7-9). This fire is fanned into a flame by the word of God, the Eucharist, meditation on the passion of Jesus, healing and reconciliation, spiritual reading, prayer for the Holy Spirit, and other means of spiritual growth.

## Eyes Fixed on Heaven

John of the Cross teaches that this one single consuming desire will galvanise us towards our ultimate goal. Since there are many conflicting desires in the heart, we must be purified of any inordinate longings, so we can be for God alone. As the psalmist prays, "In God alone is my soul at rest; my help comes from him. He alone is my rock, my stronghold, my fortress: I stand firm" (Ps 62:2-3). And again, "I say to the Lord: 'You are my God. My happiness lies in you alone'" (Ps 16:2). All the many desires of the heart need to be subordinate to this one passionate longing for God. If they are sinful desires they must be broken. If they are not sinful, they must be used totally in the service of this one goal.

The pure of heart have their eyes fixed on heaven while still being fully engaged in the earthly project. They have an eternal perspective and make all their major decisions in the light of eternity. They are not fooled by the perspective of the world which focusses solely on the pleasures and opportunities of this life which passes so quickly. They pray with the psalmist, "Lord, grant me to know the shortness of life that I may have wisdom of heart" (Ps 90:12). The desires for pleasure, power, prestige, status, and wealth do not dominate them, but neither do the desire for success, a good job, a happy family, a pleasant holiday or any other thing that this world can offer. Every desire finds its appropriate place subjugated to the fundamental passion for union with God.

John, the evangelist, gives us this perspective:

> See what love the Father has given us that we should be called children of God; and that is what we are......but what we will be in the future has not yet been revealed. What we do know is this: when it is revealed we shall be

like him, for we will see him as he is. And all who have this hope in him ought purify themselves, just as he is pure (1 John 3:1-3).

The pure of heart see God. Our journey here on earth is one of progressive purification. This means dealing with sin. John says that when we confess our sin "the blood of Jesus purifies us of sin" (1 Jn 1: 7-9). He tells us that all that the world has to offer, "lust of the flesh, lust of the eyes and pride of life" could never come from God. And all that the world craves for is coming to an end. Those who do the will of God will live forever (cf 1Jn 2:16-17).

# The Curé of Ars

St Jean Marie Vianney (called the Curé of Ars) was ordained a priest on 13 August 1815 in the chapel of the Seminary at Grenoble France. He was born 29 years earlier in Dardilly near Lyon. As a young boy he fell in love with Jesus, and at his first holy communion he was filled with an irrepressible desire to become a priest. But everything was stacked against him; lack of intelligence, insufficient funds, a raging war, and being branded as a deserter from Napoleon's forces – a situation not of his making which turned out eventually to be providential. Overcoming huge obstacles, he was finally ordained. After an initial time in the parish of his mentor, the Curé at Ecully, M. Balley, he was appointed to Ars, a tiny remote hamlet with a population of about 200 people. The parish had been neglected and was in danger of being suppressed. As he walked through the countryside to take up his appointment he lost his way. Coming upon a small boy he asked him directions. The boy set him on the right road. "My young friend" said the priest, "You have shown me the way to Ars; I shall show you the way to heaven."[30] Since the location was the border of the parish, the Curé knelt down and prayed before making his way down to the scattered huts, the village of Ars, in the middle of which stood a very small and poor church.

This humble beginning of his apostolate tells us much about the man. He was pure of heart, and so in touch with God. His focus was clear and uncompromising. His purpose simple and unchanging – to show people the way to heaven. He immediately set about the conversion of his parish; not by a pastoral program, but by prayer and fasting. When parishioners heard the new priest had arrived they were curious. They found him in the church on his knees rapt before the Blessed Sacrament in communion with his Master. Long before dawn each day whilst Ars was still asleep, a flickering light could be seen in the cemetery that surrounded the church. It was Vianney, lantern in hand, making his way from his house to the church. Prostrate before the Blessed Sacrament he poured out his heart to the Lord. "My God" he pleaded, "grant me the conversion of my parish; I am willing to suffer anything you ask of me, only let my people be converted". He joined penance to his intercession, disciplining his body, and fasting constantly. He wanted to offer his whole life to God in union with Jesus on the Cross. His food consisted of a little dry bread and a few boiled potatoes.

While he was tough on himself he was full of compassion for his people. When he listened to them he was kind and gentle, a true father, but always ready to warn them of the dangers of sin. His sermons and catechesis were simple but compelling, because he spoke with the love in the heart of Jesus. The people began to realize they had a saintly pastor; they sensed the presence of God in him. Little by little the tiny village was transformed. The fire of love in the heart of their pastor ignited their hearts as well. Wild dancing, drunkenness and blasphemy, which the Curé condemned as dangerous for the soul, disappeared from the town. Even the most wayward young men changed their ways.

He was not afraid to preach on hell as the ultimate consequence of rejecting God, but whenever he did he had tears streaming down his face as he felt the tragedy of anyone who would suffer eternal loss. His whole life was given so that none of those in his care would have such a terrible end. His eternal perspective was acute. He was not foggy or wishy-washy about the eternal verities. Jesus said, "Enter by the narrow gate, since the road that leads to perdition is wide and spacious, and many take it; but it is a narrow gate and a hard road that leads to life, and only a few take it" (Mt 7:13-14). The Curé called his people to shake off all spiritual lethargy and to choose Christ and embrace the Cross daily; this is the way to fullness of life forever.

His parishioners were drawn to him for confession and felt the joy of repentance and God's forgiveness. He listened, for he could read their hearts before they spoke, and brought comfort and reassurance. Then the pilgrims began to arrive. News spread that in this remote village in the south of France a priest consumed by prayer and penance was speaking of God, hearing confessions, performing miracles, and guiding souls to holiness. More and more pilgrims came every year, until it was in the thousands and then hundreds of thousands. And there was no program. Simply a man given totally to God, whose heart was so pure that he saw the face of God in the morning at prayer and then radiated the face of God in his ministry throughout the long day. He once said, "the good God looks neither at long prayers nor beautiful prayers, but at those that come from the bottom of the heart". At another time he added "if we love the good God we shall pray as naturally as we take our breath. Oh, how I love to say these words first thing in the morning: 'I will do and suffer everything today for the glory of God ... nothing for the world or personal interest; all to please my Saviour!'"[31] No doubt speaking of his own experience he also said, "The saints had a liquid heart. When the heart is pure it cannot help loving, because it has rediscovered the source of love, which is God."[32]

## The Problem of Mixed Motives

Purification will mean dealing with mixed motives. Blessed are those who are free from every taint and admixture of evil! The pure in heart are those whose motives are absolutely unmixed, whose minds are utterly sincere, whose lives are totally and single-mindedly for God. Unfortunately we all suffer from mixed motives to some degree. The process of purification is long. In this endeavour, the capacity for honesty with oneself before God is important. Self-knowledge is critical for spiritual growth. That is why the use of the Ignatian practice of daily examen is very helpful. This is a simple exercise at the end of the day whereby we seek the grace of God to be able to discern clearly during the course of the day where our heart has gone; how we were influenced by the Holy Spirit and in what way we were influenced by the evil spirit.³³ Getting in touch with the movements of the heart makes us sensitive to the little compromises and resistances within us that dilute our fervour and render us lukewarm and half-hearted in our quest for holiness. We discover how much we can delude ourselves and have a duplicitous heart.

Having a good spiritual director is important to help us see things as they really are, rather than as we imagine them to be. All good spirituality begins from where we are at now, rather than from the ideal to which we are aspiring. We can look at the lives of the saints and want to emulate their spiritual growth, and this is good. However, the danger can be that we create an imaginative fantasy world, mistakenly thinking our canonisation is not far away, and failing to face the reality of our poor broken hearts which need so much healing. This healing can only begin when we are honest in our self-perception. This truth will set us free. There is no one who is without mixed motivation. The difference is that some see it, and work on it. While others fail to see it and so do not grow.

## Hypocrisy, the Enemy

The "heart" in biblical thinking is the deepest region of the human person from which flows all thoughts, intentions, decisions, attitudes, emotions and behaviour. Jesus constantly called for a change of heart; to turn from attachment to sin and the ways of the flesh, and turn to holiness and the ways of the Spirit. Hypocrisy is the great enemy of purity of heart. We have seen earlier how the word hypocrisy originally meant "play acting". The hypocrite is not authentic, but puts on a show which is not the truth of who they really are before God. Jesus makes it clear that what determines the purity of an action is not the actual praying, fasting, or giving alms, since the Pharisees actually did these works. The problem was their intention. They wanted to look good before others. It is the intention of the heart which matters; that is why we should not trumpet our good works before others to gain their applause, but keep them secret, and our reward will be in heaven (Mt 6: 2-4).

We have already referred earlier to Jesus' invective against the Pharisees because they insisted on outward ritual practices but their hearts were not good. Jesus bemoans, "This people worship me with lip-service but their hearts are far from me" (Mk 7:6). They did not worship "in spirit and in truth". While their worship was technically correct according to the rubrics, their heart was not given to God. The prophet Malachi had foretold that when the Messiah came he would be like a purifying fire, which would refine the hearts of worshippers like gold and silver are purified (Mal 2:3). God does not just want correct ritual practices. He wants genuine worshippers!

When challenging the excessive attention to rituals of cleanliness, Jesus makes it clear that it is not a particular type of food that will make us unclean, but rather what flows from the heart. "It is what comes out of a person that defiles. For it is from within, from the human heart, that evil intentions come: fornication, theft, murder, adultery, avarice, wickedness, deceit, licentiousness, envy, slander, pride, folly. All these evils come from within and make a person unclean" (Mk 7:21-22). If we are authentic we will not cover up the waywardness of our hearts. We will not try to hide how divided our hearts can be. We will seek the way of purification.

The heart has a depth beyond our immediate perception. Modern psychology has helped us to understand this, but the spiritual tradition of the Church from time immemorial has upheld this reality. A mathematical image for the depth of the heart would be two asymptotes approaching one another going down into infinity. In Jeremiah the Lord says, "The heart is more devious than any other thing, perverse too: who can pierce its secrets? I, the Lord, search the heart…" (Jer 17:9). The prophet contrasts the person who trusts the Lord in a whole-hearted way with the one who puts his or her trust in earthly things. The former is like a tree by the waterside thrusting its roots into the stream, so even in times of drought he or she is without worry. The latter is like dry scrub in the desert without root and blown away in the wind. The pure in heart are those who trust totally in the Lord and they draw from the deep spring of grace that wells up within the heart to eternal life. But the truth of most of us is that while we draw from the crystal clear water of the Spirit to give life to the soul, the purity of this water has been polluted by contaminating affections and desires. This murky water must be purified.

## Active Purification

What we call the "active purification of the soul" is necessary, especially for beginners. We have to ask the power of the Spirit to break patterns of sin that keep us in bondage. We have to soak our minds in the word of God, purging them with the truth that sets us free from the illusions of the worldly mind-set. This helps us to see things the way God sees them. We must feed ourselves on the Holy Eucharist, eating the body of the Lord and drinking the blood of the Lord into sinful areas of our life. We must cleanse the heart of all selfish instincts, curbing our propensity for self-indulgence and self-glorification. We must determine to be obedient to God night and day and be like the tree planted by the waterside, drawing our life from the stream of God's grace breaking forth within the soul (Ps 1:3). We must embrace the Cross of Jesus every day by dying to ourselves and serving others (Mk 8: 34-37). In other words, all the disciplines of a genuine disciple need to be in place.

We become more "pure of heart" as we enter in the mind of Christ, and begin to grow in virtues, which are good and consistent habits of the heart, leading to qualities like Jesus. We become more one with him so that we can say with Paul, "it is no longer I who live but Christ who lives in me" (Gal 2:20). Our initial image for purity of heart was climbing the mountain of the Lord, and this holds true. But as we move more in the mind of Christ the dominant image is not so much about "going up", but rather "going down"! The mountain of the Lord becomes a descent of love! Jesus "did not cling to his equality with the Father, but emptied himself..." (Phil 2:5).

This self-emptying is the way towards purity of heart. It is the way of joining with Jesus in his humility, obedience and self-giving love on the Cross. Therese of Lisieux once said, "the more I lowered myself the more he lifted me up". She was referring to her "little way" which meant discovering one's littleness, nothingness, and total incapacity for holiness; then with this realisation turning confidently to Jesus and throwing oneself into his merciful arms. Jesus said, "Unless you change and become like little children you will never enter the kingdom of God" (Mt 18:3). Instead of trying to pull ourselves up the mountain of holiness, which is an impossible endeavour, we simply own our nothingness before God, and then in his mercy he will come to lift us up. This is the dynamic of growing in purity of heart, being formed in the likeness of Jesus by emptying ourselves, so we are fully given to God and to others.

## Passive Purification

In the spiritual life we discover at some point that after having put all our efforts into our personal transformation we are still failing dismally. The further we go towards God, the more his light shines on the soul, and the more it becomes overwhelmingly obvious that the project of personal holiness is totally beyond us. We may have given lip-service to this truth beforehand but now the reality hits like never before. We are helpless to root out the interior flaws of our make-up, the hidden fissures in the soul, the font of sinfulness that can still erupt within us. Added to this we still hang on to petty emotional and spiritual attachments which hold us back from God himself.

Thanks be to God that in his mercy he humbles us through suffering, which can become our purification. Suffering helps us realise that we must not turn anything or anyone on this earth into a god, but must rely totally on God himself for everything. We at last relinquish the control of our lives to the Lord, and let go of the illusion that we can do it. We also find to our bewilderment that what used to work in our personal prayer no longer works at all. We are plunged into long periods of darkness, with none of the previous consolations and revelations that were previously so important to us. Strangely enough this also is a blessing since the Lord is giving us a deeper level of purification. As he opens up a darker, more mysterious contemplation in the soul, he is using this time to do some "laser treatment" on the impurities within. Just like modern surgery where a laser beam is used to eliminate unwanted defects, so the Lord, our divine surgeon, is purifying us at a depth beyond our awareness. This is what is sometimes called "passive purification". Blessed are the purified, they shall see the face of God.

## Surrender to the Lord

The purification of desires is a life-long process. By the grace of God we break with all inordinate desires, no matter how good they are in themselves. They are inordinate if they hold the heart captive and not free to go to God. John of the Cross gives us the image of a bird trying to fly, but it has a thick cord tied to its leg preventing it from rising up. The cord represents unruly desires which bring disorder to our lives and hold us back from our true purpose. But he goes on to say that even if the bird is only held by a slender thread it still cannot fly. The thread has to be broken in order to be free to fully love God and come into union with him. What holds us back could be something really petty and seemingly insignificant, maybe a compulsion for certain food, or a longing for spiritual revelations, or an inappropriate affection for someone. Whatever it is we are held bound and not free for God. By letting go we let God have his way.

Near the brotherhood house where I used to live there was a large tree near the chapel. Sometimes when the brothers were quietly praying in the chapel a flock of squawking white cockatoos would land on the tree and make an awful racket. The noise was deafening and very distracting for our prayer. If this went on for too long one of the brothers would have had enough, and would race outside screaming at the top of his head. The cockatoos would take fright and with one last flourish disappear. Silence would descend. Peace again. This little scenario can help us understand what is most important about the spiritual life. Within the heart of each of us there are many conflicting desires. They are like screeching cockatoos demanding our attention. "I want this; I want that; no it is this I want!"

You have many desires that seem to be so urgently necessary for your fulfilment. But then by the grace of God, in response to his immense love for you, one day you will be like that brother who had had enough of all this noise. You will make the decision. From deep within your heart a cry will rise as an almighty shout, "I am for God!" "I am for Jesus!". And with this act of surrender all those "cockatoos" within you will disappear, and peace will descend on the soul. As it says in Scripture, "You keep him in perfect peace, O God, whose mind is stayed on you, because he trusts in you!" (Is 26:2-3).

## Sexual Purity

A key dimension of purity of heart is growing in sexual purity. If we are enslaved by sexual passions and desires the heart cannot go to God. It's not possible to pray if we have an impure heart. We cannot raise ourselves to God, who is spirit, if we are bound by the flesh. If there is sexual disorder in our lives it is a serious barrier to intimacy with God. It is a form of blindness. Only the pure of heart see God. Those captive to sexual passions succumb to lust in the eyes. They cannot appreciate the beauty of the other person, but must grasp for their own pleasure, and use the other for their own selfish ends. The pure of heart, on the other hand, see the beauty of the other person, and celebrate this beauty as a gift from God. The pure of heart do not say "no" to the goodness of God's creation, but rather say "yes" to the inherent created goodness and dignity of the other person. Purity of heart does not develop through taboos, prohibitions and fears, but rather by attraction to goodness, beauty, and holiness.

However, to be able to say "yes" we need the power of the Spirit to say "no" to any unruly, grasping desires, which have enormous destructive potential. The chaste of heart learn the art of self-discipline. They guard the heart from any contamination. They seek to make every thought captive in obedience to Christ. If a lustful image enters the mind, they dash it against the Cross of Jesus, drawing strength from the victory Jesus has won for us. They learn to mortify their eyes. Jesus said, "If your eye causes you to sin, pluck it out and throw it away" (Mt 5:29). This is a Semitic hyperbole to emphasise decisiveness; an emphatic "no" to captivity, and a resounding "yes" to freedom. There is no half measure; no middle ground; no place for sitting on the fence.

## Free from Pornography

In the image-laden society of today we are subject to a veritable bombardment of sexual enticement from TV, billboards, magazines, videos, movies, but most of all from internet porn sites. The statistics are staggering.[34] Just to mention a few: 35% of internet downloads are related to pornography. 25% of all search engines queries are related to pornography, or about 68 million search queries per day. On average the first exposure to pornography among men is 12 years old. Nine out of 10 boys are exposed to pornography before the age of 18. The old phrase "custody of the eyes" comes to mind. The eye is the window of the soul. When a dust storm comes we close the windows to protect the interior of the house. When confronted unexpectedly with sexually explicit material, we should close the eye-lids. God gave us eye-lids to protect our souls from being invaded. He also gave us hands to be able to click off quickly an unwanted "pop up" that occurs on the computer. But more so he has given us himself. When we accept this gift of his presence within us, and let Jesus become Lord of our lives, we attain self-control which is a fruit of the Holy Spirit. We come under the control of Christ, who recreates our mind, imagination and heart. Unless we rely upon the saving power of God won for us by Jesus on the Cross, the forces working against us will be too strong for us.

It is a well attested fact that experimenting with internet porn can quickly lead to compulsion and ultimately to addiction.[35] Images quickly become implanted in the brain through a physiological reaction. A chemical called dopamine is released which leads to arousal addiction. Neural pathways in the brain are opened up that make it easier for similar visual stimuli to access this part of the mind in the future. It works like drug addiction. Prevention is better than cure. The pure in heart strive never to let their eyes fall on anything that does not give glory to God; and if perchance that does happen they immediately avert the eyes or take measures to remove themselves from the situation. Better to take an axe to your computer than to become a slave to sin.

The great tragedy is that porn sex distorts what is God's beautiful gift to us. It desensitises the user to the beauty of sexuality. Our sexuality is a relational gift; we make a gift of ourselves for the other. The language of porn is the exact opposite. It is about self, orgasm, perfect bodies, bizarre titillation, and illusory sexual availability. It treats the other as a commodity, taking selfishly with nothing to offer. It is an escape from real relationship, creating a false intimacy which never satisfies. Sadly, because of this, it renders those hooked on porn incapable of genuine, healthy committed relationship. Who will save us from this mess? Thanks be to God for Jesus Christ, our Saviour. Certainly those addicted will need counselling and the help of an accountability partner, and a willingness to own the problem and the desire to be free. But let us not forget the words of Paul, "If by the Spirit you put to death the misdeeds of the body you will live" (Rom 8:13). We need to call upon the Lord to make us pure of heart. It is a fruit of the Spirit, not just of our own efforts.

St Augustine had an enormous struggle trying to be chaste. He knew he didn't have the strength to be pure. He thought it relied upon his own efforts. For a long time he agonised over his sexual addiction. Then one day, as a result of his mother's prayers, in a state of inner torment, he was prompted to pick up the Scriptures and read "Let us cast off the works of darkness and put on the armour of light; let us conduct ourselves becomingly as in the day.... But put on the Lord Jesus Christ, and make no provision for the flesh, to gratify its desires" (Rom 13:13-14). In that instant he received the grace to do it. "The light of confidence flooded into my heart and all the darkness of doubt was dispelled". Later, as he came to know the Lord more he lamented that he had not genuinely cried to God for help sooner. He said to the Lord, "you would certainly have granted me this if with the groans of my heart I had begged it of you and with firm faith had thrown my worries upon you". He knew now that all he needed to do was to cry to God with trust ,and persevere in praying, "Lord, you want me to be pure; well then, grant what you want, and then ask me what you will."[36] This is a prayer which all of us can make.

# A Life Given to God

Charles de Foucauld, who was born in 1858, grew up under the care of his wealthy grandfather. Family tragedy had made this necessary. It meant he was provided for in abundance, but he was still a troubled child. At the age of 17 he became quite rebellious. He later confessed, "At seventeen I was all egotism, all vanity, all impiety, all desire for evil; it was as if I had gone mad."[37] He remembered, "I was so free, so young. There remained not a trace of faith in my soul."[38] He went to a Military Academy and joined the French Foreign Legion. When his grandfather died he inherited the family fortune. He plunged into an indolent, self-indulgent life-style, wasting his family's money on dissolute living. He took his mistress with him to Algiers, but this flagrant lapse of discipline did not impress the Army and they sent him home. Undaunted Charles returned to Algiers and with extraordinary courage decided to explore Morocco, which was forbidden territory for Europeans. For a year under the guise of being a mendicant rabbi he chartered the whole territory, returning to France as a hero of scientific exploration. The new found glory didn't matter to him. But something was stirring in his soul.

While in the Muslim world he was deeply impressed by their commitment to prayer and the obvious devotion with which they prayed. A close friend, realizing he was on a spiritual search, suggested he go to Abbe Huvelin, the priest in charge at St Augustine's in Paris.[39] Charles approached the priest when he was hearing confessions. Without kneeling he murmured, "Father, do not be surprised. I do not come for confession. I do not have the faith. I only wish to learn some things about the Catholic religion". Father Huvelin asked, "You do not have faith. Have you never believed then?" Charles replied that he did thirteen years ago. But now he can't believe due to so many obstacles – the dogmas, miracles and all the rest. Inspired by the Spirit Fr Huvelin said, "You are mistaken, my son. What is missing now, in order for you to believe, is a pure heart. Go down on your knees, make your confession to God, and you will believe." Charles protested, "But I have not come for that!" The priest insisted, "That does not matter. Go down on your knees and say the Confiteor." Without really understanding what was happening to him, Charles knelt and confessed for a long time, covering his entire life. With the absolution from the priest Charles felt an indescribable joy and peace. His doubts were gone. His conversion was sudden and total. He said later, "As soon as I came to believe there was a God, I understood that I could do nothing else but give my life for him alone". This was the purity of heart that the priest had promised him.

Charles was so full of the Holy Spirit that he wanted to join religious life immediately. Fr Huvelin held him back for three years. Then Charles chose the most severe and demanding calling, to become a Trappist monk in a remote Syrian location. He loved the life of poverty and austerity, but he was still restless for more. Having had a pilgrimage to the Holy Land he was captured by the hidden life of Jesus in Nazareth, a way of poverty and self-abandonment. After seven years he gained permission to leave the monastery and pursue a life in Nazareth as an anonymous servant. He lived unobtrusively in a garden shed in the grounds of the Poor Clare convent close to the house where Jesus lived with Mary and Joseph. His days were spent working with his hands and most of all before the Blessed Sacrament in the convent chapel. Charles was wanting to be one with Jesus by seeking the lowest place, the least place:

> To embrace humility, poverty, renunciation, abjection, solitude, suffering, as did Jesus in the manger. To care not for human grandeur, or rising in the world, or the esteem of men, but to esteem the very poor as much as the very rich. For me, to seek always the last of the last places, to order my life so as to be the last, the most despised of men.[40]

After being persuaded to become a priest, Charles felt called to go to "the most abandoned of all people", those whom he had encountered in Morocco and the Algerian Sahara. He asked and obtained permission to go to Beni Abbes, a little oasis in the Algerian Sahara on the borders of Morocco. There he lived in a hermitage making friends with the local people and spending hours lovingly before Jesus in the Blessed Sacrament. He always slept in his tiny chapel, on the step of the altar near the tabernacle, "like a dog at the feet of its master".[41] He led a rigorous life of prayer and work, seeking to befriend his Muslim neighbours who quickly warmed to him and recognized him as a holy man of God. They were drawn to him, knocking on his door many times throughout the day, seeking for provisions but also for love. He asked his friends back in France: "Pray that the tiny atom that I am may do among these millions of souls, who have never heard of Jesus, the work he has sent me here to do."[42] He dreamed of founding a congregation which would carry this spirit of Nazareth, but no one came to join him.

Then Charles felt drawn to go even further into the remote desert region to live amongst the Tuareg people. It was the first time the Blessed Sacrament had come to the Tuareg land. He would pray before Jesus, "Sacred Heart of Jesus, radiate from the depths of this tabernacle on the people who are around you without knowing you! Enlighten, direct, save these souls whom you love!" He painstakingly translated the gospels into the Tuareg language. He settled in Tamanrasset, the only European for hundreds of kilometres, "very happy to be alone with Jesus, alone with Jesus." After ten years of this solitary life celebrating Mass every day in his hermitage he still had not one single conversion. In December 1916 Charles was fatally shot in the head by Senoussi bandits while they were ransacking his compound. Charles had always spoken of a consuming desire to identify fully with Jesus: "It is at the hour of his supreme self- annihilation, the hour of his death, that Jesus has done the most good, that he has saved the world."[43] Charles' lonely death in the desert far from friends and loved ones by his own choice of self-abandonment was his moment of most intimate union with Jesus: "Unless a grain of wheat falls to the ground and dies, it remains but a grain of wheat, but if it dies it yields a rich harvest" (Jn 12:24). Today as a result of his self-offering there are eleven religious congregations and seven associations comprising thousands of members throughout the world. The prayer of abandonment which Charles wrote a few months before his death sums up what we mean by a "pure heart":

> Father, I abandon myself into your hands.
> Do with me what you will
> Whatever you may do, I thank you:
> I am ready for all.
> Let only your will be done in me
> and in all your creatures.
> I wish no more than this, O Lord.
> Into your hands I commend my soul;
> I offer it to you
> with all the love of my heart,
> for I love you, Lord,
> and so need to give myself,
> to surrender myself into your hands,
> without reserve,
> and with boundless confidence,
> because you are my Father.

# 7
# BLESSED ARE THE PEACEMAKERS

*Blessed are the peacemakers, for they will be called children of God   Mt5:9*

The word used for peace-makers (*eirinopoioi*) suggests those who work for peace, or make peace. This work must begin with ourselves, but will not be complete until it involves action beyond ourselves, maybe beyond our comfort zone, to help others find peace. The work for peace is not only to preach the good news, nor only to help others to forgive in the heart, but also to facilitate genuine reconciliation with one another. When discussing the beatitude on mercy I insisted on the imperative to forgive. This is the pathway to peace, but fullness of peace is only found in a much more difficult task, the work of conflict resolution, when opposing parties are genuinely reconciled. We only have fully the peace that Jesus won for us on the Cross when we are able to walk again with one another. I want to show firstly how all genuine peace comes from Jesus as a divine gift. Then I will talk about inner peace as a pre-requisite for being peace-makers. After that I want to focus upon reconciliation as such. Finally, I want to underline the gospel call to non-violence when seeking peace.

## The Gift of Peace

St Paul often starts his letters with the greeting "grace and peace." He knew how much his communities needed the grace of God, through the power of the Spirit for hearts to change and peace to reign! Peace is the gift of Christ. "He is the peace between us" (Eph 2:14). The original rebellion of humanity against God dislocated our relationships with one another and also our relationship with ourselves. From the beginning there has been endemic discord and an incapacity to mend the problem. The Hebrew word for peace is *"shalom"*, and it promises restoration of harmony between humankind and God, and hence harmony with one another and within our own interior life. This is symbolised by the dream of peace even amongst the animals: "The wolf lives with the lamb, the panther lies down with the kid….the infant plays over the cobra's hole… They do no hurt, no harm" (Is 11:6-8).This *"shalom"* which the prophets promised has come in Jesus; the promise of this peace is summed up in all that the Messiah will bring: "How beautiful on the mountains are the feet of him who brings good news, who heralds peace, brings happiness, proclaims salvation" (Is 52:7).

True peace came into the world with Jesus. The background to the infancy narrative in Luke suggests a contrast between the child born in a stable in Bethlehem and the all-powerful Caesar Augustus, the Emperor, who was praised by his subjects as "the saviour of the universal human race", and as a great "peace-maker" or "bringer of peace". These claims were hollow and without any solid basis. No genuine peace can be established by political domination and force of arms. The true "bringer of peace", Luke proclaims, is Christ who had no army but was a defenceless baby coming among us in humility and love. The angels announced his arrival, "Glory to God in the heavens and peace on earth to all men of good will" (Lk 2:14). This was not wishful thinking, or something they longed would happen some time in the distant future. It was a solemn declaration with great joy that Peace had already definitively arrived on the earth, and he is the only universal Saviour, Christ the Lord. This is clearly a fulfilment of the prophet Isaiah's words: "For there is a child born for us, a son given to us and dominion is laid on his shoulders; and this is the name they give him: Wonder Counsellor, Mighty God, Eternal Father, Prince of Peace. Wide is his dominion in a peace that knows no end" (Is 9:6-7).

The new covenant is the "covenant of peace" (Ezek 37:26) and the good news is "the gospel of peace" (Eph 6:15). In the early Church this is how people greeted one another, wishing peace, the gift they desired most. This continues in the Mass today when the greeting "Peace be with you" is repeated often by the priest in the name of Jesus, and we pause before Holy Communion to greet one another with the the same greeting and a sign of peace. This is the message that we preach: "Whatever house you go into, let your first words be, 'Peace to this house!' And if a man of peace lives there your peace will go and rest on him" (Lk 10:6-7).

## Interior Peace

Jesus gives us the peace in his own heart. His first words to the apostles, when he appeared to them in the upper room after his resurrection, were "Peace be with you!" He bestowed on them what he had won for them on the Cross. He had entered into the awful darkness, alienation and lostness of sin, which cuts us off from God and from one another, and leaves us interiorly disordered. From that place, in solidarity with us, he rose from the dead. He had promised he would bring this peace to us. To emphasise the gift, after breathing the Spirit on them, Jesus repeats, "Peace be with you" (Jn 20:21). At the Last Supper before his passion he anticipated this resurrection gift in saying, "Peace I leave you, my own peace I give you, a peace the world cannot give. Do not let your hearts be troubled or afraid" (Jn 14:27-28). Note that Jesus promised "his *own* peace"; the peace in his own heart. When we accept Christ into our hearts we find true peace that surpasses all understanding. It is a peace the world cannot give. Not even a good counsellor, or a professional masseur, or soothing music, or the comfort of a loved one can minister this peace which is from Christ himself.

I cannot emphasise enough that the world's search for peace will be found in Christ. This means dedicating ourselves to quiet contemplative prayer, resting with the Beloved, the one who knows and loves us most. Through silently being with Jesus, tranquillity and order come to the soul, especially when this prayer is before the Blessed Sacrament. There is a struggle in being alone with God; but in this time of solitude, resting in the loving arms of the Lord, the heart becomes still and all is well. It is not a matter of seeking consolations but of seeking the God of all consolation. It is not so much about big revelations or emotional highs, but rather about gazing upon him with love, and more importantly allowing him to gaze upon you. Even if you inadvertently doze off, all is not lost because you are there with a purpose, and your Divine Lover is gazing upon you. If you give over the controls to him he will surprise you with his love and he will instil his gift of peace into your heart, which is his very own peace. If your heart is troubled and you carry deep resentments, or you are wounded by conflict, and wonder how you could be healed, spend time every day in a quiet chapel before the Blessed Sacrament, being real about your broken state before God, and allow the divine healer to touch your wounds with his mercy and love. In the sunshine of his love you will find restoration.

With Jesus we find that the hardness of our hearts melts and we begin to trust him with our lives. As one of Dante's souls in Paradise says, "In His will is our peace". Yes, when we trust and surrender to his loving provident care of us, we find a tranquillity in the soul that will surprise us. We ought to ask the Lord to help us. As Paul assures, "There is no need to worry; but if there is anything you need, pray for it, asking God for it with prayer and thanksgiving, and that peace of God, which surpasses all understanding, will guard your hearts and your thoughts in Christ Jesus" (Phil 4: 6-7). I keep Teresa of Avila's prayer close to me at all times:

> Let nothing disturb you;
> Nothing frighten you.
> All things are passing.
> God never changes.
> Patience obtains all things.
> Nothing is wanting to him
> who possesses God.
> God alone suffices.

## Peace through Reconciliation

God himself is the supreme peace-maker, and so are all the sons and daughters of God, because we imitate God in his peace-making; we resemble him and do what he does. Peace is who God is and what he does. Where God reigns there is peace.

God's work for peace is achieved by "reconciliation". Paul tells us, "All this is from God who reconciled us to himself through Christ and has given us the ministry of reconciliation; that is, in Christ, God was reconciling the world to himself, not counting their trespasses against them, and entrusting the message of reconciliation to us" (2Cor 5:18-20). This reconciliation means that now we can have a right relationship with God if we open our hearts to Christ, and we can have a right relationship with one another if we open our hearts to one another, and we can have interior harmony as well because of Christ within us. This is the power of love which can change the world. No longer are we doomed to be caught up in a cycle of violence against one another, but in Christ all enmity can be put to death, and we can walk together in peace. This is God's desire for us, and if we are living together according to his will we can find this peace with one another. Paul says, "God was pleased… to reconcile to himself all things, whether on earth or in heaven, by making peace through the blood of his Cross" (Col 1:20). This is his purpose. We just have to cooperate with his will and take hold of the gift available to us.

Pope Francis defines "peace-makers" as those who do not ignore conflict nor run away from it. Rather they are people who admit the conflict, own their part in it, and face into the hard work of reconciliation.[44] Nor are "peace-makers" those who become so embroiled in the conflict that they are not capable of seeing their own fault, and place all the blame on others. James warns us, "Remember this, my dear brothers: be quick to listen but slow to speak and slow to rouse your temper; God's righteousness is never served by man's anger" (James 1:19). We need to search out good teaching about how to go through conflict resolution towards mutual forgiveness and restoration of relationship.

## Conflict Resolution

My own experience of conflict in relationship, and the many times I have mediated between people in conflict, has led me to conclude that our biggest problem is being able to really listen to one another. Because one party is boiling with justifiable anger over what has happened, he or she has a hard heart and cannot hear the perspective of the other person. Mediation almost always involves helping the participants to really listen to one another and not dismiss too quickly what the other is saying. It is also important not to come to the dialogue angrily laying judgements on the other. It is best to avoid "you" statements and voice "I" statements instead. Rather than making judgmental statements that provoke the other it is best to share how you feel about the situation. This creates the space for the other to respond. You need to express your feelings assertively but not aggressively. We should avoid all global statements, such as "you always..", "you never.." and stay with the concrete issue at hand. Never stomp out, or give the silent treatment as punishment. See it through to the finish, working hard to love even though it hurts. When we recognise a fault, even if it is not as great as the other's offence, it is good to repent immediately. This gives the other person the space to repent also. If it is proving impossible to solve between the two of you then seek mediation from a mutually trusted mentor. With the grace of God, and the openness of both parties, reconciliation is possible.

## A Rwandan Reconciliation

In the Rwandan genocide in 1994, Hutu militia went on a rampage against Tutsi people. Within three months at least 800,000 innocent people were slaughtered.[45] Alice Mukarurinda, separated in the wild confusion from her husband Charles, was sheltering her baby girl, trying to hide by the river from the marauding gangs with machetes. But now the attackers were upon her. She was praying desperately that she and her baby would be overlooked. But there was no mercy. A militia man grabbed her bible and the baby from her hands and walked away. Another man came from behind her and clubbed her skull leaving a jagged wound that would never fully heal. Then from amongst the assailants Emmanuel Nkayisaba appeared before her. He had gone to school with Alice. He asked, "Do you know me?" She replied "Knowing you is not important to me. Get on with your job". She closed her eyes as Emmanuel cut off her right hand. He swung the machete again, this time at her face. She could hear her cousin screaming that the baby was dead. They had chopped her in half. A spear went through Alice's shoulder and she passed out. Miraculously she was rescued later by other survivors and regained consciousness three days later.

As she recuperated Alice was reunited with her husband who had been thrown into a dam to die but had also survived. He nursed her back to health. But she was plagued with the image of the man who had struck her. She prayed to God to show her the person who did this to her. Otherwise she would be judging everyone. Meanwhile Emmanuel was full of remorse for what he had done. He was so overcome with grief that two years later he handed himself into the police. He was thrown into prison, and during that time he wrote out his confession, even though the authorities were not interested. As a Hutu he had been forced by the militia to kill his own villagers since that was the policy during the slaughter. He was released from jail in 2003 under a reconciliation scheme, administered by *gacaca* community courts, that offered sentence remissions to genocide perpetrators who repented. He then threw his energies into the *Ukuli Kganza* reconciliation program which helped victims of the genocide to recover.

Emmanuel was shocked when he found Alice coming to the *Ukuli Kganza* meetings also. She had come to a stage of recovery where she wanted to help victims as well. He recognized her straight away with her stumped arm and large scar on her temple. But surprisingly Alice did not recognize him. She would sometimes look quizzically at him at meetings wondering where she had met him before, but the penny did not drop. Emmanuel so much wanted to confess to her but he could not bring himself to do so. Eventually a couple of years later he gathered up the courage. When they came face to face he dropped to his knees, too choked up to say anything. A friend had to speak for him. He confessed everything, making no excuses, and begged her forgiveness. She was too stunned to reply. She simply went home. But in the days following she prayed to God for help. A week later she had made up her mind. She returned to him and said, "I forgive you, and may God forgive you also". She knew she had to forgive in order to release him from his guilt, but also to release herself from her hate. Now they continue to work together for Rwandan reconciliation. Alice is the treasurer of the committee. Emmanuel is the vice-president. They talk softly like old friends, at ease and comfortable with one another. They share a common work to help all the survivors and perpetrators to be healed through forgiveness and reconciliation.

## The Mayor and the Bishop

When someone is truly holy their presence, and their words, breathe the power of peace and reconciliation. Towards the end of Francis of Assisi's life the bishop and the mayor of Assisi were at enmity with one another.[46] They were not talking with one another and were arguing with each other in public. Their quarrel was not edifying for the people and had degenerated into name calling and bickering which disturbed Francis' spirit. Being a man of peace he sent two of his brothers to go to the mayor and to the bishop, requesting a meeting with them. So, in the entrance hall of the bishop's palace, Francis, the bishop, and the mayor all came together. A small crowd gathered also, curious to see what would happen. When the saint gave the signal the friars began to sing. Everyone listened intently to the lyrics and the music which broke the silence of the vestibule. The Friars were singing the now famous Canticle of the Creatures, but they added an extra verse composed by Francis for the occasion:

> All praise be yours, my Lord, through those who grant pardon for love of you;
> Through those who bear sickness and trial.
> Happy those who endure in peace.
> By you, Most High, they will be crowned.

Francis did not address the mayor or the bishop directly. He did not try to argue with them or exhort them to change their hearts. He simply called them together to share in this prayer which had grown out of his contemplation. The mayor and the bishop looked at each other with tears in their eyes, laying aside their pride and opening up their hearts. They embraced one another and made amends. God is never so close to us and we are never so close to God than when we forgive another, and let go of the suffering caused by the conflict. The bishop and the mayor had never been so close to God as in this moment of reconciliation, which brought peace. By the grace of God they could walk again with one another. True peace had been restored.

The letter of James gives us an apt description of major hindrances to peace. "For where jealousy and selfish ambition exist, there will be disorder and every vile practice." But when we receive wisdom from on high this will bring a "pure, peaceable, gentle" spirit open to sincere dialogue and full of mercy. "And the harvest of righteousness is sown in peace by those who make peace." (James 3: 16-18). Every effort to make peace begins with personal conversion of heart. If we resist the prompting of the Spirit and harden our hearts reconciliation is thwarted and peace cannot be attained. Peace, as we know, is not just the absence of violence, nor only a wary co-existence. Rather it is achieved through the humble work of repentance and forgiveness and the patient effort over time of restoring trust that has been lost. Only when we walk again together in love through genuine reconciliation has peace fully arrived.

## Towards Peace through Non-Violence and Love

Soon after proclaiming that peace-makers are blessed children of God, Jesus gave his teaching on non-violence: "You have heard that it was said, 'An eye for an eye and a tooth for a tooth'. But I say to you, offer no resistance to one who is evil. When someone strikes you on the right cheek, turn the other one to him as well." (Mt 5: 38-40). As we saw earlier when reflecting on forgiveness, we must not add to the violence in the world, no matter how justified we may feel. If someone strikes me and I retaliate, then this will lead to an act of counter-violence from my opponent, which will in turn draw me into the endless spiralling cycle of violence. Jesus challenges us to meet the initial attack with love. He wants us to draw upon the power of his Cross, on which love conquered hatred and goodness conquered evil. That is why he commands not only to love those who do good to us, those whom we like and find pleasant, but also to love our enemies, and to do good to those who hate us, and to those whom we find obnoxious. This is not a love based on feelings but a decision to will the best for the other person, to genuinely want them to flourish, and to act accordingly. It means recognizing the intrinsic dignity of the person who is assailing me or causing injustice in my life or in some way making my life miserable. Rather than seeing the other as trash, Jesus calls us to recognise their inherent dignity. No matter how rotten their behaviour, we must choose to act with kindness towards them. This does not mean allowing the other to walk over the top of us, but at times it may mean allowing them in the short term to have the upper hand, knowing that in time God's love will have the victory.

## Turning the Other Cheek

Robert Barron has a thought provoking interpretation of the call to "turn the other cheek".[47] He suggests that Jesus' instruction is not asking us to passively acquiesce to the power of violence. In the society of the time one would never use the left hand for human contact since it was considered unclean. To slap another on the right cheek would necessarily have meant using the back of the right hand, just like a master would slap a servant or someone considered a social inferior. To "turn the other cheek" meant to prevent the slap to happen again. It gives a clear message to the aggressor that you refuse to go down the path of violence, but it also mirrors back to the violent person the injustice of what he is doing. As Jesus says we do not resist violently the one who is evil, but at the same time we can hold our ground and convey a clear message that confronts the aggressor with their injustice.

Barron offers a few contemporary examples.

Mother Teresa in Calcutta went one day with a small, hungry child to a bakery to beg for some bread. The baker rebuked her and spat in her face. She replied, "Thank you for that gift to me, now do you have anything for the child?" It shamed the man into the charitable response. During the apartheid era in South Africa, Bishop Desmond Tutu, when he was still a young priest was making his way along a raised narrow walk-way to avoid slogging through the muddy street. He was confronted by a white man coming towards him. Someone had to give way. The white man sneered, "Step aside, I don't make way for gorillas". The priest replied, "I do", and happily stepped into the mud. It wasn't that the priest was deliberately calling his assailant a gorilla. In giving way he refused to be violent, but he still confronted white man with how ludicrous his racist attitude was.

In 1979 Pope John Paul II visited his Polish homeland. The communist authorities were nervous, but they allowed the celebration of Mass in Victory Square in Warsaw. All the government officials were present as the Pope celebrated the Mass before a crowd of hundreds of thousands. During his homily the Pope preached on God, freedom and human rights – topics the communists did not want to hear. The people kept interrupting his homily shouting in unison, "We want God, we want God, we want God!". The Pope began to speak again, but they shouted all the louder for a good fifteen minutes, "We want God, we want God, we want God!" The Pope just turned to the official platform where the communist leaders were and gestured as if to say, "Do you hear?" Communism at that moment was dead. The game was up. And it was not long afterwards the entire Soviet Communist empire crumbled without a shot being fired.

## The Revolution of Love

Martin Luther King showed that non-violence has the power of love. A revolution of love will be lasting. But if we trust in arms we will always be in danger of someone starting a counter revolution. There was a story that was part of the literature of the southern blacks in the United States during the fight for racial equality.[48] Tom, a young, teenage Alabama "negro" had dared to go into a public toilet which was exclusively for whites. He thought no one was around and he needed to relieve himself. But just as he finished his business he heard the sound of boots outside, the boots of a large white man, called "Jim" in the story. Too late to escape. Big Jim was blocking his way, eyes icy with rage. One kick sent Tom to the ground, and then he fell with his face in the urine. "You break the law, nigger, and that is what you get!"

The words of Martin Luther King: "Now Tom, you have two choices before you, and I will tell you what they are, because I have suffered a lot myself for the cause of negro liberation. The first choice is that you can run out of that toilet with hate in your heart and intensify that hate tomorrow amongst your friends of your own race. You can say to yourself and others, 'The day will come when we will destroy Jim.'

But there is another choice, a more difficult one, and I, Martin Luther King, draw your attention to it in the name of the revolution of love. Get up, Tom, and recognize the smell of that filth, which is the common filth of humanity, the smell of Christ's blood, defiled with spittle on the way to Calvary. Know that Jim is more ignorant than cruel. He is not aware of the evil he is doing, but he will be one day. Forgive him, Tom, in the name of Jesus, forgive him. It is so much easier to take revenge. The difficult thing is to love, and you must love. The society we are building for tomorrow needs the binding cement of love. We cannot go on living with a knife in our belt forever. Tomorrow we will have to live with Jim, and Jim will understand us then as we understand him. You, Tom, must build your future with the power and the violence of love."

## Free from the Scourge of War

From the gospel injunction of non-violence it is imperative for the Church to pray and work for peace, so that the world can be "free from the ancient bondage of war".[49] Wars are caused so often by inbuilt injustice, excessive economic or social inequality, envy, distrust and pride. The Church is called to be peacemaker. We preach the good news of peace and try to mediate between warring parties. Pope John Paul II made the telling remark that every war is a loss for humanity. No one really wins. We all lose whenever there is war which tears apart the fabric of our human communion. We know that peace amongst ethnic groups at enmity with one another and reconciliation between nations at war will only come through conversion of hearts. Ultimately only when individuals open their hearts to the peace won by the Jesus on the Cross will we be saved from the scourge of war.

Unfortunately, the threat of war constantly hangs over the human race. The multiple manifestations of the mystery of iniquity throughout the world today is the heritage of our fallen state. But we know that Christ has come as our redeemer. On the Cross he vanquished violence. The power of evil has been decisively broken. Christ is risen! His victory over the powers of darkness is accomplished. The cry of Jesus on the Cross "It is finished!" resounds through history. The redemption of humankind has come. Even in the face of what Pope Francis has called a "third world war" being enacted in piece-meal way through random global terrorism we do not despair. We live in the sure hope that the time will come when the words of the prophet Isaiah will be fulfilled: "they shall beat their swords into ploughshares, and their spears into pruning hooks; nation shall not lift up sword against nation; neither shall they learn war any more" (Is 2:4).[50]

# 8
# BLESSED ARE THOSE WHO ARE PERSECUTED

*Blessed are those who are persecuted for righteousness' sake,*
*for theirs is the kingdom of heaven* Mt 5:10

## A Missionary Life

This beatitude is as relevant today as it was in the early Church. Jesus warned his apostles, "If the world hates you, remember that it hated me before you.... A servant is not greater than his master. If they persecuted me, they will persecute you too" (Jn 15: 18-20). From the beginning of the Church the proclamation of the good news met with intolerance, hostility, persecution and martyrdom. Jesus predicted, "You will be dragged before governors and kings for my sake, to bear witness before them and the pagans" (Mt 10:18). Reading about St Paul's missionary life, we are left in no doubt about how true this prediction was. Paul was mocked, reviled, imprisoned, beaten, stoned, and finally beheaded. These sufferings were for Paul a great blessing. He found them to be the very means of deepening in his love for Jesus, since it gave him the privilege of reproducing in his own life the pattern of Jesus' passion and death (Phil 3:10).

Paul received the revelation from the Lord, "My grace is enough for you; my power is at its best in weakness". Being assured that the Lord works most powerfully through his vulnerability to suffering at the hands of others, he said, "that is why I am quite content with my weaknesses, and with insults, hardships, persecutions, and the agonies I go through for Christ's sake. For it is when I am weak, then I am strong" (2Cor 12: 9-10). He declared confidently: "These are the trials through which we triumph, by the power of him who has loved us" (Rom 8:37). Paul had indomitable hope no matter what obstacles came against him, or how often he was hounded by others, and attacked because of his faith: "We are afflicted in every way, but not crushed; perplexed, but not driven to despair; persecuted, but not forsaken; struck down, but not destroyed; always carrying in the body the death of Jesus, so that the life of Jesus may also be made visible in our bodies" (2Cor 4: 8-11).

Paul not only found blessing through the suffering he personally endured, but he also used his sufferings at the hands of his enemies as a witness and encouragement for others. He wrote to Timothy, whom he was mentoring:

> You have observed my teaching, my conduct, my aim in life, my faith, my patience, my love, my steadfastness, my persecutions, and suffering the things that happened to me in Antioch, Iconium and Lystra. What persecutions I endured! Yet the Lord rescued me from them all ... Indeed all who want to live a godly life in Christ Jesus will be persecuted (2Tim 3: 10-13).

Paul is not glossing over the inevitable consequences of following Jesus. It means certain persecution. But he is inviting Timothy to look at his own witness to Christ in the face of the opposition that he has experienced. Rather than lose heart when we are harassed by others and persecuted because of our faith and way of life, we are challenged to take hold of the blessing.

## To Die with Jesus

In the early Church the ultimate ideal for holiness was to be identified with Jesus in his suffering and death, and so come into his resurrection. The most radical way to do this was to die a martyr's death. Even before they were executed, while they were still in prison, the martyrs-to-be were revered as holy intercessors who were already close to God. This was because they were soon to have the privilege of dying in imitation of Jesus. They were truly blessed, because as Paul said, "the suffering we endure in this world is nothing compared to the glory yet to come" (Rom 8: 18).

When Luke told the story of the first martyr, Stephen, he deliberately described his death as modelled on that of Jesus (Acts 7:55-60). Like Jesus, Stephen was arrested and dragged before the Sanhedrin. As with Jesus they put up false witnesses against him. As with Jesus he stood before them totally innocent of the charges. As with Jesus, Stephen cried out, "I can see heaven thrown open and the Son of man standing at the right hand of God". When they ran to stone him Stephen cried out, "Lord Jesus, receive my spirit", in imitation of the Master, who had uttered the last words, "Father into your hands I commend my spirit". And as with Jesus, during his last agony, Stephen forgave his persecutors. Down through the centuries Christian men and women have taken the same path, and in the strange manner of God's providence the times of most severe persecution have been the times of flourishing growth in the faith. As Tertullian was famously to observe, "The blood of martyrs is the seed of Christians".

## Persecution Today

Some people live in the illusion that persecution and martyrdom belong to a previous age, left behind with the Romans throwing the Christians to the lions, or with the later missionary priests and religious who gave their lives for bringing the good news of Jesus to countries where Christianity was not present. Mistakenly people can think that since Christianity is now so widespread, and the churches are so seemingly powerful, martyrdom is not really an issue. This is a common narrative in the Western world, but in fact it is totally false. While estimates differ, most reputable agencies estimate that a Christian is killed for their faith somewhere in the world every two hours. The Vatican spokesman for the United Nations Human Rights Council in May 2013 claimed that as many as 100,000 Christians are martyred each year, and that the trend is increasing rather than diminishing.

The most vulnerable to being killed for their faith, or for values derived from their faith, are the two thirds of the 2.3 billion Christians in the world today who live in dangerous situations, often poor, and belonging to ethnic, linguistic and cultural minorities. Both political and religious persecution of

Christians is rife. It is estimated that about 10 percent of all Christians suffer persecution. But it is not only in the more dangerous areas that Christians are persecuted. According to the Pew Forum, Christians face harassment in a total of 139 countries, representing almost three quarters of all nations on earth, including many where Christians are a strong majority, such as Mexico, the Philippines, Columbia and South Sudan.[51] Anywhere Christians openly profess their faith, take a public stand against obvious injustices, or simply put themselves in harm's way because of the imperative to proclaim the gospel, they are at risk. Christians are the most persecuted faith group in the modern world.

## Modes of Persecution

Christians today suffer from many forces bent upon their destruction in many different situations. Sadly a large proportion of this is perpetrated by religious bigotry. In Sri Lanka in 2009 hot-headed Buddhist monks attacked Christian churches and other targets across the country. In India Christians are often attacked by Hindu radicals, such as the outbreak in 2008 in Orissa which led to over 300 churches and nearly 6,000 Christian houses reduced to ashes or damaged rendering more than 56,000 people refugees in the jungle. In this persecution more than 100 Christians were martyred for their faith, and hundreds of others were tortured for refusing to renounce their faith. Most of those murdered were given the choice: renounce Christ and become Hindu and you live; otherwise you die. They chose Christ. The rise of radical Islam with terrorist groups such as the Boko Haram in Nigeria and the so-called Islamic State in Syria and Iraq, has accelerated Christian persecution to an alarming level. Anti-Christian persecution is a disturbing reality in other Muslim states as well, such as Afghanistan, Saudi Arabia, Somalia and Iran. Beheadings, torture, rape, kidnappings, mass killings, forced starvation, imprisonment and even crucifixions attest that the persecution of Christians did not end at the foot of the cross or at the gates of the Roman Colosseum.

One of the most chilling episodes of Islamic persecution was the 2015 kidnapping and beheading of 21 Egyptian Coptic Christian migrant workers in Libya. On February 15 a five minute video was published showing the beheading of the captives on a beach along the southern Mediterranean coast. A caption in the video called the captives the "people of the cross". As in other Islamic State videos, the captives wore orange jumpsuits, intended as a retaliation for the treatment given prisoners in Guantanamo Bay. Many of the men could be heard chanting the words "Lord Jesus Christ", while some screamed the name of Jesus in their final moments. Almost immediately Pope Tawadros II, the head of the Coptic Church, declared the men martyrs. Pope Francis gave his endorsement of the martyrdom, and the Catholic bishop Antonios Aziz Mina of Giza said, "The name of Jesus was the last word on their lips. And like the early church martyrs they entrusted themselves to the one who would receive them soon after. That name, whispered in the last moments, was like the seal of their martyrdom." Beshir Kamel, whose brothers Bishoy and Samuel were among the martyrs slain by the group, said that his siblings' martyrdom serves as "a badge of honour to Christianity". He continued, "ISIS gave us more than we asked when they didn't edit out the part where the martyrs declared their faith and called upon Jesus Christ. ISIS helped to strengthen our faith."

The witness of these men calling on the name of Jesus just before being beheaded was a clear sign that ISIS will ultimately fail. No amount of carpet bombing will destroy ISIS because it is an ideology in which young people are taught to live by hate, a cult of death, which destroys the human soul. But the witness of life of those Christians who imitate the love of Jesus, confessing his name, is invincible. Through the Cross of Jesus love has conquered hate and goodness has conquered evil. The ideology of totalitarian communism finally fell under this spiritual power, and so will the ideology of ISIS. The only thing in doubt is how long it will take.

In October of 2015, 100,000 Christians fled the Iraq city of Mosul in one night after the jihadi fanatics embarked on a genocidal campaign of ethnic cleansing. When Jihadi fighters took the predominantly Christian city they summarily tortured and killed the families who spoke out against them, and took girls as sex slaves who they used for barter amongst themselves. Mosul's entire population was given a 24-hour ultimatum to either convert to ISIS's radical brand of Islam or face beheading. Those who chose to stay behind had to pay a heavy tax of roughly the amount of a year's normal wages or be executed. Before 2003 there were about 2 million Christians in Iraq. Now there are only about 180,000. These are sobering statistics, but while severe persecution may deprive people of their home and country and render them desperate refugees, it cannot rob them of hope in the risen Christ, still carrying his wounds to assure them that he is with them in their suffering and that like every other ideology of hate in human history ISIS will not have the last word.

In addition to the rising religious persecution Christians are suffering also under totalitarian states such as China and North Korea, and from ultra-nationalistic groups such as in Turkey, and also from organized drug cartels in countries such as Colombia and Mexico, as well as from state-imposed security policies such as in Israel where check-points restrict visits of Christian families between East Jerusalem and the West Bank, and where social restrictions make it difficult for Christians to survive.

## Professing the faith boldly

The memory of the martyrs, and the very real opportunities for martyrdom today, stir within us a desire to unashamedly proclaim the faith boldly and be prepared to accept the consequences. We walk in the great tradition which produced martyrs such as Ignatius of Antioch, a courageous bishop, fearlessly longing to face the lions in the Roman arena, so he can share in the suffering and death of Jesus. "I am yearning for death with all the passion of a lover. Earthly longings have been crucified; in me there is left no spark of desire for mundane things, but only a murmur of living water that whispers within me, 'Come to the Father'."[52]

We can also think of the Jesuit missionary, Isaac Jogues, one of the North American martyrs. After having been taken captive by the savage Mohawk Indians he was held as a slave for a number of years, but always keeping his heart fixed on Jesus. Isaac and his fellow Jesuit prisoner, Rene Goupil, made a pact that they would die with the name of Jesus on their lips. Isaac was so delighted when he heard Rene utter the name of Jesus as he was being clubbed to death by an angry brave. After escaping from the Mohawk camp Isaac arrived back in France, but only to beg his superiors to let him return. He was something of a celebrity in his home country because he visibly carried the wounds of torture on his body. But worldly glory was not for Isaac; he longed to glory in the Cross of Christ. After much hesitation his superiors finally allowed him to return, only to be captured almost immediately again. This time he was subjected to torture and a cruel death. True to his promise Isaac died with the name of Jesus on his lips.

The martyrdom during the French revolution of sixteen Carmelite nuns of Compiègne on July 17, 1794 remains an inspiring memory for all Christians. They were herded into two of the five open carts taking victims from the Conciergerie prison to the guillotine; all along the way they sang the *Miserere,* the *Salve Regina* and the *Te Deum.* Upon arrival at the base of the guillotine, they sang the *Veni Creator.* Before climbing the scaffold each nun renewed her vows, kissing a small terracotta statuette of the Madonna and Child held by the Prioress, Mother Teresa of St Augustine. They went to their deaths one after another singing the *Laudete Dominum.* The Mother Superior, by her own request, was the last to be executed. Only when her head fell did the singing stop, and there was silence. These nuns were examples of tranquility and serene confidence in God. They forgave their executors and prayed for their salvation. Mother had a premonition two years previously that the execution would come upon them, and she spent these years preparing her sisters for the worst. She encouraged them not to fear dying for Christ, but to offer themselves as a sacrifice to God so peace can come to the world. During their imprisonment they composed a canticle for their martyrdom to be sung to the familiar tune of the Marseillaise. The first verse runs:

> Give over our hearts to joy, the day of glory has arrived.
> Far from us all weakness, seeing the standard come;
> we prepare for the victory, we all march to the true conquest,
> Under the flag of the dying God we run, we all seek the glory;
> Rekindle our ardour, our bodies are the Lord's,
> We climb, we climb the scaffold and give ourselves back to the Victor.

## God-Given Courage

Would you have the courage to offer your life for the sake of Jesus? None of us can answer that question definitively. The story of the Carmelite martyrs was re-told by Francis Poulenc in his 1957 opera, *Dialogues of the Carmelites*. Poulenc included in the story a fictional nun, Blanche of the Agony of Christ, a young aristocratic girl, who fled the convent terrified of the prospect of martyrdom, but returns at the final scene, gathering the courage to climb the scaffold singing the last verse of the *Veni Creator*, and then dying with her companions. Her very real struggle reminds us of Jesus himself in the Garden of Gethsemane agonising over the imminence of his passion. He says to his disciples, "the spirit is willing, but the flesh is weak" (Mt 26:41), but then he says resolutely, "Rise, let us go forward" (Mt 26:46).

Remember Peter who was willing to go to prison and die with Jesus. Then a few hours later he crumbled under the keen eye of a servant girl, and denied the Lord. In the flesh, like Peter, we would not be capable of joining Jesus in his suffering. But by the grace of God we could. All we can say honestly is that we trust God we would not fail; that in our weakness God would be our strength. After genuine repentance and experiencing Pentecost Peter was unstoppable in his heroic witness of the good news, and finally was martyred in Rome. We trust that when the opportunity arises, despite our frailty and vacillations, we would also be anointed with the Spirit and stand for Jesus. A story I once heard illustrates this challenge.[53]

It was Sunday morning in a little chapel on the border of Venezuela and Colombia. As Mass was beginning a band of guerillas armed with machine guns came out of the jungle and blasted their way into the chapel. The priest and the congregation were terrified. The men dragged the priest out and machine gun fire was heard. They knew he had been executed. The chief of the guerillas came back into the chapel and addressed them, "Anyone else believe in that Jesus stuff?" There was frozen silence. Then a young man stood up. "I love Jesus" he declared. They summarily dragged him outside. Gunshots again. Another gone. The leader returned. "Anyone else?" Several others came forward and professed their faith. They also were driven outside, followed by the sound of the machine gun fire. When there were no more people willing to identify as believers in Christ the guerilla chief came back into the chapel and ordered the remaining people to get out: "You have no right to be here!" And he herded them out of the chapel. To their great surprise standing outside were the priest and the others who had professed their faith. The chief ordered those people and the priest back into the church. To the others he warned angrily, "Until you have the courage to stand up for your beliefs you don't deserve to be in there. You stay out here". Then the guerillas disappeared into the jungle.

Put yourself in that little chapel faced with decision, what would you have done? Would you have stood for Jesus?

## What is Martyrdom?

The overall picture in the world today is grim and quite sobering for budding Christian missionaries. There are few places in the world which are now relatively safe to do missionary work. Many witnesses of the faith every day are prepared to put their lives on the line for the gospel. But we need to ask what constitutes a martyr? Does a Catholic priest working in a dangerous area who is robbed and shot dead in his presbytery without any opportunity to profess his faith beforehand qualify as a martyr? It depends on how wide we choose to define it. The word "martyr" is from the Greek word meaning "witness". So in broad sense we are called to be "martyrs" every day. Through giving of ourselves in love for the sake of Jesus and for others we are witnessing to the love of God and as followers of Jesus each day are called to die with and for Christ. But how does the church define someone who is to be revered as a saintly martyr?

We can approach this question by noticing the difference between Matthew's and Luke's account of this beatitude. Luke has Jesus say, "Blessed are you when people hate you, drive you out, abuse you, denounce your name as criminal, *on account of the Son of Man.*" The emphasis here is on witnessing through faith in Jesus. The persecution is because of the Son of Man. This suggests that the disciples will suffer and die for their faith in Christ. The reason for the persecution is *"odium fidei"*, hatred of the faith. Historically, this has been the usual way of establishing who is a martyr.

However, in more recent times, the Church has broadened its understanding. This broader definition is justifiable especially since Matthew's version says, "Blessed are those who are persecuted *for the sake righteousness.*" This suggests that martyrs are not only those who die for professing their faith, but also those who lay down their lives for self-giving love, like Maximilian Kolbe, the Polish priest who in Auschwitz Nazi prison camp offered himself to be sentenced to death in the starvation bunker in place of a married man with children. Martyrs are also those who give their lives in defence of the oppressed, such as Archbishop Oscar Romero, as we saw in a previous chapter. In addition those who die to safeguard their virtue can be considered martyrs, such as Maria Goretti, who resisting the sexual advances of a young man preferred to be knifed to death rather than to accede to his demands. Even in the nineteenth century we have an example of this type of martyrdom. In 1886 Charles Lwanga and his 21 companions were martyred for their Catholic faith in Uganda. But the real issue which caused their deaths was the refusal of these page boys to accede to the perverse lustful demands of the young king. These examples indicate that it is possible that the Church may go even further in defining martyrdom, as long as it involves standing for Catholic faith and morals.

What attitudes characterise a true martyr? Who are the ones the gospel says are blessed because they are persecuted? What qualities of heart do they have? Even though a necessary factor is that the person is a heroic witness to Catholic faith and morals, of itself this is not sufficient. Those who engage in violent resistance are not genuine martyrs. Jesus makes it clear that it is better to flee if necessary rather than to fight (Mt 10:23). Nor are those who abuse their persecutors true martyrs. It is not enough to die for one's faith in Christ or for righteousness, if it is without love. Paul says as much: "If I give way all I have, and if I deliver my body to be burned, but am without love, it will gain me nothing" (1Cor 13:3). As we have seen it was with forgiveness on his lips that Stephen died. One is not made a martyr by the amount of suffering endured, but by the cause for which one suffers. But it cannot be any cause; it must be in the cause of love. A sign of authenticity will always be forgiveness on the lips of the martyr.

## Love your Enemies

In May 1996 the GIA, a radical Islamic group in Algeria, kidnapped seven Trappist monks in the Atlas mountains and held them hostage, demanding release of several of their companions from the French government. When the French refused, the GIA killed the monks by slitting their throats. All of France was horrified. Catholic churches throughout France tolled their bells at the same time in honour of the monks' death. Two years before this atrocity happened the Prior of the monastery, Dom Christian de Chergé, had a mysterious premonition that he would die at the hands of extremists. He wrote a letter forgiving his future assassins, sealed it, and left it with his mother in France. It was only opened after his violent death. It read in part:

> If it should happen one day- and it could be today- that I become a victim of the terrorism that now seems to encompass all the foreigners living in Algeria, I would like my community, my church, my family, to remember that my life was given to God and to Algeria; and that they accept that the sole Master of all life was not a stranger to this brutal departure.
>
> I would like, when the time comes, to have a space of clearness that would allow me to beg forgiveness of God and my fellow human beings, and at the same time to forgive with all my heart the one who will strike me down...
>
> My death, obviously, will appear to confirm those who hastily judged me naïve or idealistic: "Let him tell us now what he thinks of it!" But they should know that ... for this life lost, I give thanks to God. In this "thank you", which is said for everything in my life from now on, I certainly include you, my last-minute friend who will not have known what you are doing ... I commend you to the God in whose face I see yours. And may we find each other, happy "good thieves" in Paradise, if it please God, the Father of us both.

## Persecution in Secular Society

Another type of persecution faces Christians especially in Western countries which is not by force of arms or due to fundamentalist religious hatred or by any of the avenues already mentioned. It is more deadly to the faith, since it is more hidden. Without exaggeration, we could argue that witness to Christ was easier in the early Church, and also in persecuted churches today, than it is in a society that purports to support Christianity, but by its cultural mores is in fact hostile to the gospel. In the early Church, at least it was easy to know where you stood. When the Emperor's officials arrived in the village and dragged out an effigy of Caesar, demanding all people burn incense before it, your options were obvious. Either compromise your faith and burn incense to save your life, or refuse to do so for the sake of Jesus and seriously jeopardize your chances of remaining alive much longer.

Similarly, when Islamic militants invade your town and put before you the choice, either convert to Islam or die, you have a blatantly clear choice, and the consequences are obvious. In contrast the persecution today in Western society is more subtle, but a massive challenge to the faith. Rather than the faith being attacked by the sword, it is threatened by secular ideology, public opinion and the hostile propaganda of many media outlets. The secularized culture regards Christianity as outmoded, unenlightened, irrelevant, and of no use to the human project. I suggest this context may well generate a new type of martyr.

## Religious Freedom

The issue in Western countries is becoming focused on religious freedom for Christians. Pope Benedict warned of a "dictatorship of relativism", meaning that in this so-called "enlightened" society no adherence to absolute moral truths can be tolerated. This means that Christians, who by definition hold to absolute beliefs and values, can only be tolerated as long as they keep to their private lives and personal worship, but they don't have a right to enter public debate with their peculiar convictions about what is good for humanity. In fact the "dictatorship" quickly becomes one governed by the secular elite and politically powerful, who consider it their duty to rid the society of any vestige of Christian presence, and to preserve the society from being further contaminated by Christian beliefs and practices. We have unfortunately seen the emergence of this trend in recent years, and it will call for Christians to be courageous in standing for the truth in love. Some may be called to pay a high price in this.

Some may disagree that this problem comes under the rubric of "persecution" since no one's life is being threatened. However, if genuine religious freedom is curbed, even if churches are not being torched or practicing Christians physically attacked, it would seem persecution is an apt description. Religious freedom is not just freedom to go to church on Sunday and pray at home.[54] Religious freedom means we have the right not to be coerced into silence by name-calling and accusations, for example in the debate about what constitutes a true marriage. Religious freedom means that the church has the right to provide health care, schools, orphanages, child care, social welfare, in a manner that is consistent with our beliefs and values. The government or secular pressure groups do not have the right to insist "we like your work with vulnerable women; we just need you to offer them abortion as well" or "we like your schools, but we can't allow you to teach that marriage between man and woman is a more truly human union than any other sexual union". It is also religious freedom for the church to have the right to employ for her services, such as schools, hospitals, universities, and welfare agencies, people who will uphold the Catholic beliefs and values.

## No "Persecution Complex"

As we face the growing hostility toward Christianity in the secularized world we must avoid falling into an unnecessary "persecution complex", feeling that everyone is unfairly against us, and retreating into a defensive huddle. A more humble stance recognizes that in some ways we have failed as a Church. The sexual abuse crisis underlines this dramatically. Public opinion has shifted against us at least to some degree because of our own lack of credibility. People who admire Christian principles are scandalized by our failure to live them well. Maybe also we have failed in our efforts to communicate the faith. Often the Church is perceived as judgmental and condemning, rather than welcoming and merciful. I opened up this issue when earlier reflecting on gentleness. In facing opposition we need to have the attitude encouraged by Paul, "when reviled we bless; when persecuted we endure; when slandered we try to be reconciled" (1Cor 4: 12-13). The letter to Diognetus speaks of this approach amongst the early Christians, "They love all men, but are persecuted by all ... they are reviled, and they bless."[55]

It is good to take note that Jesus says, "Blessed are you when men revile you and persecute you and utter all kinds of evil against you *falsely* on my account" (Mt 5:11). The inclusion of the word "falsely" indicates that maybe sometimes the accusations are actually true and just, and sometimes not so. Not all hostile words spoken against us are untrue or unjust. So not all accusations render us blessed. We need to be open to criticism and ready to receive correction, even from our "enemies". The secular anti-religionist protagonists often have something to teach us. The exposure of significant sexual abuse in the church is an obvious example. While some may be attacking the Church with evil intent, many are simply calling the church to account for the sins of its members.

The blessedness of the persecuted links with that of the meek, since the way to meet opposition is always with a gentle spirit. We must not succumb to paying back our persecutors in a vengeful way. As Paul advises, it is better to meet evil with goodness, and hatred with love, in imitation of Jesus crucified. By meeting the attack with kindness we "heap red-hot coals on their head", which means that if they have any decency their faces will burn with shame for the way they have behaved (Rom 12: 19-21). This beatitude also links with "blessed are those who mourn", since we weep over those who hold vendettas against the Church, or launch vitriolic attacks against us. This is a weeping of love and mercy, deeply sorrowful to see people rejecting God, or acting in ways that God abhors, even if it is in the name of God. It is a genuine love for our enemies and a readiness to forgive them for their violence against us.

## Persecution in the Family

A highly emotionally charged arena of persecution for Christians can come in one's own family. Jesus predicted this. Paradoxically he said, "Do not suppose I have come to bring peace on the earth; it is not peace I have come to bring but a sword" (Mt 10:34). What can he mean by such a claim? We have already professed that Jesus is the "Prince of peace", and the peace-maker par excellence. Is this talk about bringing a sword a contradiction? Luke's account helps us understand, since Jesus says he came to bring "division" rather than the sword. This gives us the clue for an answer to the problem. In both accounts Jesus then goes on to speak about division in the family, "For I have come to set a man against his own father, a daughter against her mother, a daughter-in-law against her mother-in-law." Because of our adherence to the gospel, we can find ourselves divided from our closest relatives and loved ones. Jesus calls each one to decision. This can unfortunately mean sometimes separation from a loved one, or at least a distancing that cannot be easily overcome. To live the gospel in a secular climate where many of our siblings or parents have rejected the faith can call for heroic sacrifice. When others in the family are indifferent to the faith or even hostile to it, we are called to a deeper love.

Some experience a persecution from members of their family which cuts deeply. Again we can see the close connection with "Blessed are they who mourn". Through their decision for Christ and his Church many have "lost" loved ones. They silently weep over those who have rejected Christ and his Church, and they long to share the beauty and truth of their faith with their parents and siblings; but it is not yet possible. Like St Monica they are called to shed bitter tears as she did for her son Augustine, believing all the while that God would bring about the impossible.

## The Joy of Persecution

It is a safe assumption that the church will always experience persecution, no matter what shape it takes. But we should not feel daunted by this prospect. There is nothing more joyful than sharing the good news of Jesus. Rejection will come our way. We will be mocked and ridiculed, but many will open their hearts to the love of God. Here is the consolation. It is worth the trials and tribulations to experience the joy on the faces of those who come to know Jesus. It is no accident that the Church is growing rapidly in many places where it is experiencing persecution. This is part of the blessing that Jesus promises. "Those who sow with tears will reap with songs of joy" (Ps 126:5). In times of travail Jesus promises that the Church is guaranteed to be the place where the kingdom of God is taking hold in the hearts of many. Jesus promised his Church "the gates of hell will not prevail against it" (Mt 16:18). This means that even though we are weak and powerless, the proclamation of the good news of Jesus will break through the strongholds of darkness and win hearts to the love of God. Wherever the Church is present, even as a tiny group of disciples in a remote missionary field, she is an effective sign of the Kingdom of the love, joy and peace which has come through Jesus crucified. When she is under persecution she is fulfilling her calling most radically. When she is suffering insults and violence in union with Jesus, by the mysterious providence of God, her mission is most effective.

This last beatitude is an invitation to follow Jesus, the crucified Christ. During the persecution that broke out against the church in Kandhamal in northern India in 2008 Fr Thomas Chellan and Sr Meena Barwa were captured. Fr Thomas narrowly escaped being burnt alive. Sr Meena was stripped and raped, and then both were forced to begin what they later called their "crucifixion parade". Half naked they were forced to march through the crowd while being beaten with sticks, crowbars, axes and spears, and spat upon, cursed and reviled in foul language. They were forced to endure this humiliating "Calvary walk" for half a kilometre. Later they reflected on this experience in the light of faith and could find the blessing. Sr Meena said, "Jesus is alive on the Cross and still suffering in our people. I thank God for using me to face this humiliation and giving me the chance to suffer for the people of Kandhamal." Fr Thomas said, "Love is a sacrifice and to sacrifice for love's sake is a joy" He attests to the truth that the way of the Cross ultimately brings lasting joy. The witness of these two living martyrs served to strengthen the faith in the households of thousands of Christians who are facing every day the tensions of the Church's mission in northern India. No catechetical program or pastoral formation could have been more effective in galvanizing their faith response and eliciting a courageous witness to the good news of Jesus.

# Beatitudes As A Whole

The reader will have noticed that there is considerable overlap in meaning between the different beatitudes. They are profoundly interconnected. For example, the poor in spirit have humility which makes them gentle of heart. Those who mourn over the world may well suffer persecution. The pure in heart, who long for God, are also the one's who hunger and thirst for righteousness. The gentle who meet violence with love are also peace-makers. The peace-makers build on the forgiveness of the merciful. Those who do works of mercy care for the hungry. Given all this connectedness, is there some way we could give a unified vision for the beatitudes?

I have deliberately avoided trying to unify the beatitudes by a theological or psychological systematization. Any attempt to do this would fail, because it would do violence to the scriptural revelation. Nevertheless, I think it is good to consider the beatitudes as a whole. So as a way of concluding my reflections, I want to suggest a number of ways we could do this.

## The Heart of Jesus

Firstly, and most significantly, each one of the beatitudes is a window into the heart of Jesus. Their unity is established in Christ, since they are his fundamental attitudes of life. Anyone who is growing in Christ should also be growing in these attitudes, and exhibiting them in their way of life. The beatitudes show us the way of Jesus. If we take the way of Jesus we are blessed. This has been the main theme of our reflections.

Ultimately the way of the beatitudes leads to the Cross; each beatitude is perfected in the heart of Jesus crucified. Gazing upon Jesus on Calvary, as he hangs on the Cross, we find the meaning of love, what it is like to give oneself completely to the will of God, and to offer oneself totally for the sake of others. Here we see the beatitudes in their most poignant expression. Stripped of everything, he is the poorest of all; his heart broken open for the world, he weeps for the lost; refusing to retaliate, he is meek and humble of heart; crying out "I thirst", he longs for righteousness in the hearts of all; being totally innocent before evil assailants, he is purity itself; forgiving the good thief he is rich in mercy; shedding his blood he brings peace and reconciliation; despised and rejected, abused and persecuted, he accomplishes the kingdom.

## The Kingdom Actualised

Another closely related unifying feature of the beatitudes is that Jesus speaks of belonging to the kingdom of God. The first and the last beatitudes explicitly promise the kingdom. The poor in spirit are given the kingdom of God. Their humility and littleness allow entry into the kingdom. As Jesus said, "Unless you change and become like a little child you cannot enter the kingdom of heaven" (Mt 18:13). Those persecuted for their faith radically share in the passion, death and resurrection of Jesus, which accomplished the kingdom. They are kingdom people. These two beatitudes, the first and the last, provide the framework around which the whole proclamation is presented. The promises attached to the other beatitudes are simply ways of saying the same thing. Those who mourn shall be comforted in the kingdom. Those who are gentle shall be instruments of bringing the kingdom to the ends of the earth. They shall "inherit the earth". Those who hunger and thirst for righteousness shall be satisfied in the kingdom. Those who are merciful shall have mercy shown them when the kingdom is brought to completion at the last judgment. Those who are pure in heart are experiencing already the joy of the kingdom, which is seeing God, and are destined for the beatific vision in heaven. Those who are peace-makers are already called sons and daughters of God, heirs to the kingdom, which they experience now but not yet in fullness.

As we saw earlier, Jesus began his ministry with the proclamation of the kingdom, "The time has come. The kingdom of God is upon you. Repent and believe the good news" (Mk 1;15). The core of his message was that the reign of God's love has broken into the world in a definitive way. The world can never be the same again. The Saviour has come and his kingdom will last forever. In preaching the beatitudes Jesus is announcing what his kingdom is like. It is not like the realm of an earthly ruler. It is not a realm at all. Rather it takes hold in the hearts of people by the grace of God as they grow in his attitudes of heart. It is a rule of love which was inaugurated by his ministry of preaching and healing, accomplished by his death and resurrection, and now becomes actualised as the beatitudes are lived by his disciples.

## The Anointing of the Spirit

Another thread that unites the beatitudes is the anointing of the Holy Spirit. This is more implicit. To be "blessed" is to be an "anointed one". In Luke's gospel Jesus stood up in the Synagogue at Nazareth, opened the scroll of the prophet Isaiah, and read, "The Spirit of the Lord has been given to me, for he has anointed me" (Lk 4:18). He was referring to his baptism in the Jordan when the Spirit came down upon him. To live the beatitudes, we need to be "anointed ones". This happens initially in baptism and confirmation, and is renewed as we surrender more to the anointing. We can say with Jesus, "The Spirit of the Lord has been given to me, for he has anointed me". Under this anointing of the Spirit, by the grace and mercy of God, we can grow in poverty of spirit, weeping for others, with gentleness in relationships, thirsting for righteousness, with purity of heart, with mercy and compassion, being peace-makers and joyful under persecution. It is all a work of the Holy Spirit.

In the introduction to the book I described something of what it means to be "blessed". We are not "blessed" because of our good works, but because of the Holy Spirit. The source of the blessedness is not our own virtuous actions, but God's merciful grace. Becoming more like Jesus is a sign that we have God's blessing on us. The original anointing comes from God's initiative, and gives us the power to change. This blessedness increases as we cooperate with the grace of God. That is why Scripture says, "The Holy Spirit is given to those who obey him". So when Jesus says, "Blessed are the poor in spirit", "Blessed are the gentle" and so on, he is referring to the anointing which already exists in the hearts of those who have entered the kingdom of God, and will increase as we cooperate with his merciful grace in our lives.

## The First Disciple

Another way to unite the beatitudes is to consider the "first disciple", the Blessed Virgin Mary. She lived the beatitudes par excellence. In Mary we see how we are intended to be. We are not meant to major in one or two beatitudes and leave the rest to others. Mary shows us we need all of them for integral spiritual growth. Mary was acclaimed by Elizabeth, "Blessed (*makarios*) is she who believed that the promise of the Lord would be fulfilled in her" (Lk1:45). The reason for her blessedness is that she stood on the promise of the Lord, even when it seemed impossible.

Mary's real greatness before God was due to her "yes" to God when the angel announced she was to be the mother of the Messiah. "Let it be done to me according to your word" is the response to the Lord which each one of us needs to make ever more deeply in our lives. The surrendered heart is the truly joyful one. Mary was so full of the joy of the Lord that she imparted this joy wherever she went. When she greeted Elizabeth the child in her womb leapt for joy. Mary burst forth with a wonderful song of joy, "My soul glorifies the Lord, my spirit rejoices in God my Saviour. He has looked on the lowliness of his handmaid. Henceforth all ages shall call me blessed" (Lk 1:46-48). Here again the Greek word for blessed is "*makarios*". She is exulting in heavenly joy which the true disciple knows when living the beatitudes. This is the joy of being Christian.

Mary is the "*poor one*" of God. In her *Magnificat* she is full of gratitude that the Lord has looked upon her lowliness, her nothingness. She is "*gentle woman*" with not a harsh word for anyone, but has a heart ruled by the love of God. Mary *weeps with Jesus* for humankind, standing at the foot of the Cross; her heart broken with Jesus for the world. The *Stabat Mater*, a 13th century hymn, conveys Mary's sorrow:

> At the cross her station keeping
> stood the mournful Mother weeping,
> Close to Jesus to the last;
> Through her heart his sorrow sharing,
> All his bitter anguish bearing,
> Now at length the sword has passed..
> Christ above in torments hangs;
> She beneath beholds the pangs
> Of her dying glorious Son.

Mary *hungers and thirsts for righteousness*. She knows the arm of the Lord will "scatter the proud hearted" and "cast the mighty from their thrones" and raise up the lowly. She *proclaims "his mercy is from age to age"* and he "protects Israel his servant, remembering his mercy which was promised by our fathers". Her *heart is pure*, having been born without sin and never sinned. All the more reason why in her song of gratitude she rejoices in God's mercy. She speaks the *word of peace* to Elizabeth stirring the child in the womb. And the *sword of affliction* pierced her heart, as she shared in the humiliation of her Son at the hands of Roman soldiers.

## Our Broken Humanity

Another unifying factor is our own broken humanity, in which Jesus shared fully, without sinning. Jesus does not speak down to us from on high, but speaks to our hearts from his own experience of human weakness and suffering. He knows the chaos and mess of our lives and how we find it so impossible to put things together well. We hear the call to "become perfect as my heavenly father is perfect", but we find ourselves failing miserably. We know the Lord says "be holy as I am holy", but we seem weighed down by lethargy, half-heartedness, and recurring patterns of sin. In this situation of weakness we can feel the beatitudes are splendid ideals far beyond an ordinary Christian, and maybe designed for outstanding saints and martyrs, but not for us.

How can I be gentle when my irrational anger rises up in me? How can I weep with others when I know how self-centred I am? How can I thirst for goodness in my life or that of others when I am plagued with self-seeking temptations? How can I be merciful and forgiving when judgments and resentment keep my heart oppressed? How can I be pure of heart when my many desires are warring amongst themselves? How can I be a peace-maker when the history of my relationships is so bruised and damaged? How can I stand firm under persecution when I am so timid about my faith and fearful of the consequences? These are realistic and challenging questions that have no trite answer.

However, could it not be that underlying these questions there is a hidden arrogance and pride? They sound as if everything depends on us, and little on God. We fall into despair if we are only looking at our fallen humanity and not looking at the Lord who saves us. In fact it is a great grace to encounter the crassness of our human state and the poverty of our true condition before God. Rather than despair we need to turn to the only one who can rescue us. St Paul, experiencing the same anguish of inner turmoil cried out, "Who can save me from this wretched state?" And the answer came, which has echoed down through history, "thanks be to God for Jesus Christ our Lord!" (Rom 7:24).

The fundamental need is for each of us to be brought low, to come to that place where we are deeply convinced of our utter nothingness without God, and our total incapacity to do anything towards our sanctification without his saving help. Looked at from this perspective, "poverty in spirit" is the fundamental beatitude of all, since all the other beatitudes require this level of humility and detachment for them to be realized in our lives. Jesus says, "Blessed are the poor in spirit", that is, those who know their utter helplessness to be holy, who are aware that they cannot love others as Jesus has loved, that they are easily compromised in the heart, and feel the burden of the Cross of their own sinfulness. This is, in fact, the starting point for sanctity. Rather than fall into a pit of self-pitying discouragement we need to humbly acknowledge our true state before God, and cry out to him for mercy. He cannot resist that call. He is a God who "hears the cry of the poor" and "the crushed in spirit he saves".

The blessedness of all the beatitudes depends upon knowing our inner poverty. Therese of Lisieux counselled us never to let our imperfections worry us. We become holy not *despite* our weaknesses, but *because* of them. When we own our weakness and nothingness we gain the grace not to rely on our own powers alone, but to throw ourselves confidently on the infinite mercy of God. Realizing we are nothing, we discover that Jesus is everything. She says never to become discouraged by our weaknesses and failings. Rather let them be the very means by which the Lord will redeem us. Our faults make us realize how weak and powerless we really are. Rather than condemn ourselves because of our failures we need to accept them with peace, and use them as the way towards God.

If we become down-hearted about our imperfections, we are rebelling against our littleness and inner poverty. Therese says, "the sorrow that casts us down is the heart of our self-love", and "to brood gloomily over our own imperfections paralyses the soul". When we see the truth of our compromised and duplicitous heart, we must not be dismayed, but accepting the truth, use this realization to throw ourselves totally on the mercy of God. He is our only salvation. Towards the end of Therese's life one of the sisters said to her, "you must have struggled very much to reach your degree of perfection". She replied, "It is not that at all. Sanctity does not consist in this or that practice. It consists in a disposition of heart which makes us humble and little in God's arms, conscious of our weakness and confident even to audacity in the goodness of our Father."

## A New Way of Love

Finally, I want to emphasise that the beatitudes inspire and encourage us in a new way of love. They reveal to us the heart of Jesus and offer empowerment to love like him. More than anything else we may need to do as Christians in the world today we ought to *live the good news of love*, articulated by Jesus in the beatitudes. This has power to change the world. When a community of disciples is living the beatitudes many will be drawn by the persuasive power of their love. There is nothing more attractive than the evident joy in ordinary people who genuinely love one another and reach beyond their own circle in loving others, especially those on the fringes of the society. The beatitudes proclaimed by Jesus speak of the joy in the heart of God, who is love. When they are actually lived in a loving community, this way of Jesus is irresistibly attractive. The joy of the good news of God's love is for all men and women. This resurrection joy is contagious.

The human heart is made to love. Jesus summed up his commandments in just two – firstly to love the Lord your God with your whole heart, your whole soul, your whole mind, and your whole strength, and secondly to love your neighbor as yourself. In the beatitudes he offers the fundamental attitudes which we need to be able to do this. The human heart sings with blessedness when we are loving God, and loving others.

Only God's love can ultimately satisfy the many desires of our hearts. Yet we can be tempted to think that wealth, pleasure, power or honour could satisfy. Jesus answers the propensity for *wealth* with a call to "poverty of spirit"; only by detachment of spirit and total dependence on the loving providence of God do we find real joy. He answers the craving for *pleasure* with a promise that the true blessing is with those who weep and mourn. Joy is not found in living a shallow, empty existence, addicted to "having a good time". Those who mourn are the truly blessed since they live with the pain in the heart of God for this broken world. Jesus responds to those who aspire towards having *power* over others with a call to gentleness of heart, a meekness of spirit. The meek renounce earthly power and glory and give control of their lives over to God. Rather than using their natural strength to dominate others they learn to take up towel and water like Jesus and humbly serve. The true joy is not found in taking from others but in giving until it hurts.

Jesus meets those who try to make their life worthwhile by seeking prestige, status and *honour* by promising the joy of persecution. To preach and live the gospel rarely brings accolades and worldly applause. Rather Jesus promised his disciples, "you will be hated by all for my name's sake. But he who endures to the end will be saved" (Mt 10:22). Seeking worldly honours is bad for the soul. To suffer with Jesus on the Cross ennobles the soul. Love is what conquers the world. As Jesus said, "In the world you will face persecution. But take courage; I have conquered the world!" (Jn 16:33)

The pure of heart are single-minded for God. He has so captured them by his love that their hearts burn for union with him. Nothing else will satisfy. No other ambition, no matter how good and worthy it may be, will rival this one passionate desire for God alone. Their hearts have been set on fire: "Love is a flash of fire from God himself that no floods can quench and no torrents drown. For love a man is prepared to give us all that his has and count nothing of the cost" (Song of Songs 8:6).

This love contains within it the attitude of mercy, which is love exercised most sublimely. Jesus calls the merciful blessed because this is his heart for the world. In a beautiful text in Hosea God is threatening to bring his vengeance upon Israel because of their disloyalty, but the Lord relents, "My heart recoils from it, my whole being trembles at the thought. I will not give rein to my fierce anger. I will not destroy Ephraim again, for I am God, not man" (Hos 11:8-9). In a somewhat anthropomorphic way the author is conveying to us that within God himself he has resolved the tension between his mercy and his justice. Mercy has trumped justice; mercy is paramount. His name is mercy. The Cross of Jesus speaks powerfully of this: "He was pierced through for our faults, crushed for our sins. On him lies a punishment that sets us free. By his wounds we are healed" (Is 53:4-5).

But justice is still to be sought. Blessed are those who hunger and thirst for moral righteousness. Their holiness will not only be in their faith response but also in their works. They long to see things change in their own lives, but also in society so that it is ordered towards safeguarding and honouring the dignity of each human person. They will also be peacemakers. The God of peace has won peace for us on the Cross. As we allow Jesus to become Lord of our lives his peace dwells within us, and we become instruments of peace. The prayer attributed to St Francis of Assisi comes to mind, especially since I am making the case that all the beatitudes show us the way of love. With this prayer we can fittingly conclude these reflections.

> Lord, make me an instrument of your peace.
> Where there is hatred, let me sow love;

Where there is injury, pardon;
Where there is discord, union;
Where there is doubt, faith;
Where there is despair, hope;
Where there is darkness, light;
Where there is sadness, joy;
For your mercy and for your truth's sake.
Divine Master,
Grant that I may not so much seek
To be consoled, as to console;
To be understood, as to understand;
To be loved, as to love;
For it is in giving that we receive;
In pardoning that we are pardoned;
And in dying that we are born to eternal life.

# ENDNOTES

i   *Catechism of the Catholic Church,* 1716
ii  *Catechism of the Catholic Church,* 1717
1   Benedict XVI, *Jesus of Nazareth* (N.Y.: Doubleday, 2007) p.74
2   *Catechism of the Catholic Church* (CCC), 1717
3   Pope Paul VI, *Evangelii Nuntiandi,* 21
4   See ibid., 41
5   *The Little Flowers of Francis,* 2
6   Holy See Press Office, "Message of the Holy Father to the Executive President of the World Economic Forum on the occasion of the Annual Meeting at Davos, Switzerland", 20.01.2016
7   Pope Francis, *Evangelii Gaudium* (EG), 197
8   EG, 198
9   I have chosen to put this beatitude on gentleness before the one on mourning. I favour this order, which is found in some translations, since it offers a smoother unfolding of meaning.
10  Francis De Sales, *Introduction to the Devout Life,* 3,9 (Doubleday: N.Y., 1955) p 144.
11  Ibid p 145-146.
12  Leo Sanchetin and Patricia Mitchell, A Great Cloud of Witnesses, (Washington:The Word Among us Press, 1998) pp 151-152
13  *Letters of St John Bosco,* 4,201-205
14  *Gaudium et Spes,* 1
15  Boniface Hanley, *No Strangers to Violence,* (Indiana: Ave Maria Press, 1983) pp 35-60
16  For the story related here see *Esther* 2-5
17  John Paul II, Homily at Shrine of Divine Mercy, Lagiewniki Poland, 17 August, 2002.
18  See Fr Ken Barker, *His Name is Mercy,* (Melbourne: Modotti Press, 2010) pp 137-139
19  Pope Francis, EG, 270
20  Maria Di Lorenzo, *Blessed Pier Giorgio Frassati: an Ordinary Christian,* (Boston: Pauline Books, 2004)
21  Oscar Romero, The Violence of Love: A Compilation of Quotes
22  Ibid
23  Ibid
24  John Chrysostom, Homily on Lazarus, 2,5
25  Gregory the Great, Regula Pastoralis, 3,21
26  See Fr Ken Barker, *His Name is Mercy,* (Melbourne: Modotti Press, 2010)
27  The examples here are taken from Susan Conroy, *Mother Teresa's Lessons of Love and Secrets of Sanctity,* (Huntington, Indiana: Our Sunday Visitor,2003)

28　Francis of Assisi, *The Testament*, 3
29　See Francis of Assisi, *The Little Flowers*, 25
30　Abbe Francois Trochu, *The Cure of Ars*, (Illinois: Tan Books, 1997) p 113
31　Ibid. p 200
32　Ibid. p 450
33　See George Aschenbrenner, "Consciousness Examen", *Review for Religious*, Vol.31 (1972,1) pp 14-21
34　Statistics taken from "Internet Pornography by the Numbers: a significant threat to society" www.webroot.com/au/en/home/resources.
35　See Jonathan and Karen Doyle, Choicez Media, The Problem with Pornography: A DVD resource.
36　St Augustine, Confessions, VI,11; X,29
37　Jean-Jacques Antier, *Charles de Foucauld*, (San Francisco: Ignatius Press, 1999) p34
38　Ibid. p 36
39　Ibid. p 100-101
40　Ibid. p 152
41　Ibid. p 188
42　Ibid. p 200
43　Ibid. p 324
44　Pope Francis, EG, p 226-228
45　This story by Jamie Walker, "Blood Ties", *The Weekend Australian Magazine*, April 5, 2014, pp 17-21
46　Gianmaria Polidoro, *Francis of Assisi*, (Assisi: Edizioni Porziuncla, 2008) pp 228-229
47　Robert Barron, Catholicism, (N.Y.: Image books, 2011)
48　This story told by Caro Carretto, *In Search of the Beyond*, (London: Darton, Longman and Todd, 1975) pp 143-145
49　CCC, 2307
50　See CCC, 2317 and Vatican II, *Gaudium et Spes*, 78
51　Reported in John L. Allen, *The Global War on Christians*, (N.Y.: Image books, 2013) p 34
52　Ignatius of Antioch, *Letter to the Romans*, 7
53　See William J. Bausch, *A World of Stories*, (Mystic Cn: Twenty-third Publications, 1998) p 271
54　George Pell, "The Meaning of Religious Freedom and the future of human rights", Lecture to School of Law at University of Notre Dame Sydney 22 August 2001
55　*Epistle to Diognetus* 5, 11

# OTHER BOOKS BY FR KEN BARKER MGL

## ALIVE IN THE SPIRIT
PAPERBACK, 208 PAGES, $24.95
ISBN 978-1-922168-50-4

FOREWORD WRITTEN BY ARCHBISHOP MARK COLERIDGE.

This book by is a delight; simple to read but profound in the message it brings. He draws largely on his experience of the Holy Spirit's activity in his own life, and also that of others, through the "baptism in the Spirit". I believe that this book will encourage readers to totally surrender their lives to receive what Fr Ken calls the "kiss of the Spirit". - Allan Panozza, former president of the ICCRS

## YOUNG MEN RISE UP
PAPERBACK, 260 PAGES $22.95
ISBN: 978-1-921421-06-8

Fr. Ken Barker believes in young men. He speaks into a culture in which many young men have become lost and confused in their identity. He points them towards Christ as the one who will answer their deepest questions and bring fulfillment to the profound longings of the human heart. He challenges young men, both single and married, to stand up and be counted. He is confident that through the quality of their lives and their courageous witness, young men can have a major impact for good on the Church and its mission in the contemporary world.

## AMAZING LOVE
PAPERBACK, 166 PAGES, $22.95
ISBN: 978-1921421-66-2

With an engaging blend of scriptural reflection, theological investigation and very personal and human stories of struggle, confusion and journeys in faith, Father Ken Barker has provided his readers with a very real reason to live their lives in hope.

– Archbishop Timothy Costelloe SDB – Archbishop of Perth

## His Name Is Mercy
Paperback, 148 pages, $22.95
ISBN 9781921421457

Foreword by Archbishop Mark Coleridge

"At a time when the spirit of vengeance is abroad in many ways, it is hard to think of a more important theme than mercy. Without it, human beings are destined, like Cain, to murder their brothers and sisters. But mercy takes us out of the fratricidal world into the world of love where the human being is free to become what God has always had in mind, free to be in the image of God and to share the divine ecstasy."
-- Archbishop Mark Coleridge (Foreword)

## The Wonder of the Eucharist
Paperback, 176 pages, $24.95
ISBN: 9781925138580

The Wonder of the Eucharist is for all Catholics, especially those who want to refresh their personal appreciation of this sacrament. It stimulates us to break out of the routine and formality of ritual practices, and to discover the wonderful treasure of the Eucharist which can transform our lives. -- Most Rev Peter Comensoli

AVAILABLE FROM YOUR LOCAL BOOKSTORE

or

www.connorcourt.com
www.amazon.com
www.bookshopblackwell.co.uk
www.bookdepository.com
www.barnesandnoble.com

www.ingramcontent.com/pod-product-compliance
Lightning Source LLC
Chambersburg PA
CBHW070555160426
43199CB00014B/2516